OVERCOMING
Financial
INVASION

*A Strategic Guide to
Upgrading Your Finances
in a Downgraded Economy*

Dr. Cora L. Green

Cover & Interior Book Design by Scribe Freelance | www.scribefreelance.com

ISBN: 978-0-9895443-0-6

Published in the United States of America

*This book is lovingly dedicated to my late father,
Musgrave Arnold,
and late mother,
Agatha Arnold nee Thompson,
whose words of inspiration and encouragement
still linger on
and echo sweet music in my ears.*

Acknowledgements

ABOVE ALL, I GIVE the highest praise and thanks to God. Without Him, I would be like a ship without a sail!

Sincere thanks to Dr. Faith Fredrick, Dr. Janet DiPietro, Reverend Theresa Blizard, and the entire team at Faith Christian University for creating an atmosphere conducive to the completion of this work.

Gratitude goes to Bishop Larry Chester for calling me forth and providing me with the opportunity to plan and implement financial workshops under his leadership.

Special thanks to my nephew, Daniel Middleton, III. He calmed my fears and coached me when I was clueless. As Creative Director of Scribe Freelance, he applied his innate expertise to the design of this book, from cover to cover.

I acknowledge my children Phillipa Vernon-Reid, George Vernon, and Georgia Vernon, who believed in me and cheered me on through the completion of this book.

I thank my sisters Bernice Craig, Patsy Middleton, and Rita Townes for their encouragement and numerous phone calls, when I resorted to hibernation.

I extend sincere gratitude to my friends and colleagues not mentioned, who contributed to the success of this book. I could not have made it without your support.

Last but most importantly, I owe debts of love to my special husband, Ervin C. Green, for his indispensable support, patience, understanding, and tolerance during the times when I was out of balance and spent most of my leisure time writing this book. He once stated: "I would like to make an appointment to have a cup of coffee with you." Thank you for hanging in there! Otherwise, I could not have completed this portion of my journey.

General Information

The term "financial literacy" includes the corresponding practical money skills.

The terms "financial literacy" and "personal finance" are used interchangeably.

The terms "spending plan" and "budget" are used interchangeably.

The terms "personal financial statement" and "statement of financial condition" are used interchangeably.

Listings of the tables, survey instruments, charts, and graphs can be found in the front of this book. The actual diagrams are included in the corresponding chapters.

A portion of the data used to construct the tables and charts was adapted from the reports of other authors.

Published in the United States of America.

Abstract

AS THE WORLD PLUNGED into the financial crisis of 2007, people struggled everywhere. America was not exempt from the worldwide blaze of the financial fires that quickly ignited and rapidly spread throughout the Nation. The financial catastrophe peaked in 2008. Numerous fuels that significantly impacted the financial catastrophe have been identified. One major flammable source that helped the rapid ignition of the financial fires results from a transition. The American people have traded their trust in God for a pseudo trust in material possessions. They have substituted the God of the American biblical foundational motto, "In God We Trust," with the god of materialism. Another combustion that assisted in the rapid blaze of the financial fires is the low rate of financial literacy possessed by Americans, nationwide. This deficiency has persistently plagued the nation for some time now and continues its plight. Being financially literate does not mean that individuals are financial geniuses. It simply means that individuals have been empowered with the concepts and skills necessary for sound financial decision-making, and are proficient in personal financial management. Many public and private institutions such as the Federal Government, Financial Industry Regulatory Authority, Junior Achievement, Financial Literacy and Education Commission, and the Federal Deposit Insurance Corporation acknowledge that Americans are suffering from a financial literacy education shortfall and have taken a stance against financial illiteracy. These firms have collaborated to promote such education and awareness to Americans of all ages. The goal of the promoters is to empower individuals to be able to understand the dynamics of everyday personal finance. The educators aim to increase both the number of individuals reached each year and the rate of financial literacy. They believe that by training Americans to become financially astute and know how to guard against financial pitfalls, the downgraded economy as well as the livelihood of individuals and families will be improved.

Contents

Lists

LIST OF CHARTS

LIST OF ABBREVIATIONS

Chr .... Chronicles

Cor .... Corinthians

Deut .... Deuteronomy

Ecc .... Ecclesiastes

Ezek .... Ezekiel

Gal .... Galatians

Gen .... Genesis

Heb .... Hebrews

Hos .... Hosea

Isa .... Isaiah

Jas .... James

Jer .... Jeremiah

Jn .... John

KJV .... King James Version

Lam .... Lamentations

NIV .... New International Version

Operational Definitions

Achilles' heel is a small but deadly weakness that in spite of overall strength can lead to a downfall.

Adjustable rate mortgage is a type of mortgage in which the interest rate changes (usually goes higher), on a particular date, as agreed to by the lender and the borrower. The details of the adjustments are disclosed in the mortgage note (or contract).

Alta A loan is a loan that is based on the borrower's credit score.

Annual percentage rate combines the interest paid over the life of the loan plus the total costs to obtain the loan. It measures the true cost of the loan.

Assets are things an individual owns.

Bad debt is debt that is not backed by an asset. Examples of bad debt are credit card debt, personal loans, and cash advances.

Behavioral finance is a new science that explains how an individual's emotions and reasoning affect their financial decision-making.

Broker is the middleman between the borrower and the lender.

Convenience sample is a group of individuals that are selected because they are available and easy to reach.

Debt-to-income ratio is the percentage of an individual's gross income that is used to cover debt.

Demand account is an account such as a checking or savings account from which the owner can withdraw funds at any time without giving notice to the depository institution.

Fault lines are errors or weaknesses that cause a mistake and are blamed for the mistake.

FICO score is a (Fair Isaac Company) numeric score that ranges from 300 to 850 and represents the risk of the borrower. Subprime borrowers are usually assumed to have a score of 660 or below.

Flippers are buyers who purchase real estate, remodel it, and sell it a short time later to make a profit.

Financial literacy is having the knowledge and skills necessary to process financial information and making wise decisions regarding money management.

Financially literate individuals are knowledgeable about financial matters and are able to use the knowledge they possess to make wise decisions, avoid financial pitfalls, and improve their financial situations.

Generation X refers to individuals who were born between 1965 and 1980.

Generation Y refers to individuals who were born between 1980 and 1996.

Good faith is a sincere honest intention to deal fairly with others.

Herd behavior is acting like everyone else or doing what everyone else is doing.

Housing bubble is an economic bubble that develops as a result of rapid increases in real estate values.

Interest rates reset is an adjustment to the interest rate that takes place at the end of a specified period, per the original agreement.

Liability is a debt or financial obligation – a bill that an individual is responsible to pay.

Mainstream credit is a system used by financial institutions to offer credit to trustworthy customers who possess average-to-high FICO scores.

Personal finance is the application of financial principles to money management.

Personal Financial Statement is a document that discloses a snapshot of the assets and liabilities of an individual at a certain point in time.

Practical money skills are the hands-on applications of financial literacy principles.

Pre-qualification is the process by which the lender examines the financial statistics of a borrower and tells the borrower if he or she will qualify for a loan, and the amount of the loan.

Principle is a rule or guide for conduct or action.

Prime borrowers are individuals who are considered to be credit-worthy and have a FICO score of 720 or greater.

Self-control is the ability to control one's emotions, behaviors, and desires in order to obtain some reward, or avoid some punishment.

Social pressure is a compelling force felt by an individual that persuades him or her to take certain actions. The force comes from family and friends.

Subprime borrowers are individuals with FICO scores of 660 or lower who have been late in making monthly payments, have a foreclosure or charge-off on their credit report, and a high debt-to-income ratio.

Tenet is a principle believed to be true by organizations, families and individuals.

Unbanked individuals do not have a checking or savings account.

Under-banked individuals have checking and savings accounts, but do not use the other services offered by financial institutions.

Underserved individuals are those who are not provided with sufficient banking services

Zero-down loan allows the borrower to finance the entire loan amount without putting down a deposit.

Chapter One

STATEMENT OF THE PROBLEM

A FINANCIAL CRISIS HAS IMPACTED the world. The American nation considers the crisis to be the most severe since the Great Depression of the late 1920s and 1930s. As the contagion continues to rampantly spread, concerns regarding possible deterioration of the financial dilemma soar above the norm. The fear of the disaster becoming worse continues to be almost everyone's nightmare.[1] People everywhere fearfully limit their financial activities. Some apply restraints voluntarily, while others are forced to refrain from spending due to loss of income. Many households experience feelings of unrest caused by the far-reaching effects of the financial pandemic. The impacts of the crisis cause many to struggle. The financial woes, targeted at everyone but conveniently devastating the low income and minority population who possess limited financial literacy, rampantly spread throughout many households. People everywhere are in search of relief from the strains of the catastrophe. Many who are not saved, who have not allowed Jesus to be Lord of their lives, run to the church in search of answers. They soon realize that the church is not exempt from the crisis. The financial plague has entered the church and the people of God are struggling likewise. The church resembles the world and the world resembles the church, and no one can tell the difference. Before long, the unsaved move on in a desperate attempt to find solutions to the financial problems that have engulfed their livelihoods, and many end up wandering from church, to church, to church.

While many facets with varying weights are identified as the causes of the economic crisis, this study focuses on two reasons this national, present-day pandemic has attacked so many people. For purposes of this study, the primary reason is that Americans everywhere have exchanged

---

[1] Abdul Adamu, "The Effects of the Global Crisis on Nigerian Economy," M. Sc. Thesis, Nasarawa State University, Nasarawa State. Online: http://www.rrojasdatabank.info/crisisdb/onnigeria09.pdf (10August 2011).

the supreme God of the American motto "In God We Trust," for a generic god (money). In doing so, many have moved away from the Bible-based financial culture that once governed their livelihoods and have wandered or merged into a worldly or fleshy culture based on the love of material possessions. Those who have gone astray to serve money bear fruits such as lust, greed, jealousy, anger, strife, covetousness, and hatred, among many other types.[2] Instead of seeking first the Kingdom of God and His righteousness and thereafter allowing all things to be added on, many Christians are mentally preoccupied with worldly possessions and aim to fulfill personal desires.[3, 4] As a result of the cultural exchange, many end up mismanaging their finances and experience great financial difficulties.

The secondary cause of the financial crisis is the lack of financial literacy. Although most individuals deal with money every day primarily to take care of physical needs such as housing, food and clothing, many do not possess the knowledge and skills necessary for proper financial management.[5] These two traits (financial knowledge and skills) have a hand-in-glove relationship and work together to form the tenet of successful personal financial management. Without knowledge of at least rudimentary financial concepts, individuals are unable to make informed decisions and are therefore likely to err at personal financial management.[6] Although it may not necessarily be that a child of God sins as a result of making a bad financial decision, these errors may deter Believers from accessing the promises of God.

BACKGROUND

Financial decision-making has mushroomed into an increasingly complex task that most adults are required to deal with on an ongoing basis. Two

---

[2] King James Version / Amplified Bible / Parallel Bible. Grand Rapids, Michigan: Zondervan, copyright 1987 by the Lockman Foundation. Print. I Tim. 6.10: "For the love of money is the root of all evil."

[3] Matt. 6.33: "But seek ye first the kingdom of God and his righteousness; an all these things shall be added unto you."

[4] Prov. 21.2: "Every way of a man is right in his own eyes."

[5] Hos. 4.6: "My people perish for lack of knowledge."

[6] Family Services Center, "The Need for Financial Literacy," 2004. Online: http://www.fsc-hsv.org/moneymgt-finliteracy.htm (10 August 2011).

primary characteristics necessary for making sound financial decisions are: (1) a blueprint or instruction booklet containing principles / guidelines (rules for conduct or action), and (2) the possession of at least elementary financial literacy and the corresponding practical money skills. The absence of these attributes can impede rational decision-making.

In order to live in this earth according to God's Divine plan, he has given everyone the necessary "**B**asic **I**nstructions **B**efore **L**eaving **E**arth" (**BIBLE**) to be used as a guideline. The Bible is God's manual and includes his blueprint for victorious living in this earth. One way in which God speaks to everyone is through the pages of the Bible.[7] Parents establish rules and guidelines as a form of guidance for their children, to protect them from harm. At times, parents repeat themselves when speaking to their children, to reinforce what was said. They expect their children to be obedient. Those who are disobedient face consequences. Likewise, there are times when God speaks through the Bible to his children and repeats himself numerous times. He does this for the same reasons parents do it – to discipline his children, to protect them from harm, and help them to avoid pitfalls. He desires that His children obey his instructions and adjust their behaviors. God always knew individuals would have a problem with money and therefore, his manual contains "2350 verses on financial subjects including wealth, generosity, borrowing, investing, financial planning, businesses, inheritance, taxes, purchases and possessions."[8]

Biblical principles of finance are the financial rules or guidelines that are given to everyone by God to be used for practical living. Despite reading God's principles on financial management as set forth in the Bible, many individuals continue to manage their finances according to their personal codes of behavior and fail to adhere to God's principles as prescribed in his manual. They blatantly ignore the fact that "the Bible is filled with (God's) insights and wisdom when it comes to money matters." One reason many individuals disregard the Word of God is because they do not understand who they are in Christ Jesus and are therefore unaware of their rightful privileges. As a result, they mismanage the finances that

---

[7] Prov. 30.5: "Every word of God is flawless; He is a shield to those who take refuge in Him."

[8] Brian Kluth, "Biblical and Financial Insights Into Generosity and Finances." Money Matters. Online: http://www.kluth.org/people/bookchapter.htm (18 March 2012).

God has placed in their care and end up living beneath their privileges.[9] Those in this group fail to create a personal relationship with God whereby they can experience the "abundant life" according to God's Divine protocol.[10, 11] Much too often, as a result of ignoring the wisdom of God and disobeying his Word, many individuals end up in a financial mire with only one exit – adherence to God's financial principles as set forth in his Word.

God desires that his people prosper in every area of their lives.[12] He knows all things and is aware that two main ingredients for financial prosperity are: (1) wisdom and (2) the understanding and application of his financial principles.[13] Therefore, he exhorts his people to get wisdom and understanding in all their endeavors.[14] Wisdom allows individuals to determine the best end for their finances and shows the best means to that end. Once individuals are able to envision the most profitable end for their finances and understand what actions they need to take in order to arrive at the prosperous end that has been predestined by God for their lives, they are able to find their purpose in this earth – to glorify God by living according to his commandments and principles, and get to heaven in the end.[15, 16] Possession of wisdom and understanding helps individuals to circumvent many of the destructive financial pitfalls encountered on a daily basis. However, knowing is not enough – receiving education in financial literacy will not get the job done. Individuals must take action. They must

---

[9] Ibid.

[10] Jn 10.10: "I am come that they might have life and that they might have it more abundantly".

[11] Matthew Henry. *The Matthew Henry Study Bible.* (1994 :2119). Living the abundant life means that individuals should not merely live to exist and get by, but should live a comfortable, plentiful life wherein they are happy and rejoice here and now, and enter into their eternal life wherein they will never experience death or the fear of dying.

[12] 3 Jn 1.2: "Beloved, I wish above all things that thou mayest prosper and be in good health, even as thy soul prospereth."

[13] Ps. 139.4: "Great is our Lord and mighty in power; his understanding has no limit."
Ps. 147.5: "Even before a word is on my tongue, behold, o Lord, you know it altogether."

[14] Prov 4.7: "Wisdom is the principal thing; therefore get wisdom: and with all thy getting get understanding."

[15] Jer. 29.11: For I know the thoughts and plans that I have for you," says the Lord, "thoughts and plans for welfare and peace and not for evil, to give you hope in your final outcome."

[16] Henry. (1213).

act upon the knowledge gained. Successful personal finance is the direct result of faith in action.[17]

---

[17] Jas. 2.7: "Even so faith, if it hath not works, is dead, being alone."

The Need, Purposes, and Significance of This Study

THE NEED

THE LANDSCAPE OF PERSONAL FINANCE has drastically changed and has become more sophisticated over the past decades, as a result of modern technology. As more complex financial products such as payday loans, 401(K), debit cards, an array of pension plans, and various types of mortgages continue to enter the volatile, ever-changing financial markets the level of financial literacy needed in the past for successful financial management is no longer enough. Consequently, individuals and families continue to face challenges on a daily basis brought on by the financial decisions they make. Oftentimes the details of transactions are not understood. Whereas individuals only had to choose between the interest rates of bank loans and savings plans, they are now faced with a multitude of complicated financial products from which to choose. To compound the matter, many of the financial products carry a wide range of options. For example, the responsibility of pension plan management has been shifted from the employers to the employees.[18] As a result of this change, the burden of securing one's future financial well-being comes with added concerns. One of the primary concerns is the life expectancy of individuals. Modern technology and medicine has lengthened the lifespan of individuals and people are now living longer. This creates a greater need for maximum returns on investments. In order to maximize returns,

---

[18] Dana Twight, "Getting Our Money's Worth: Exploring State Strategies for Investing in Financial Literacy Education," June 2007. Online: http://feppp.org/pdf/state-strategies.pdf (August 5, 2011). Over the last four decades there has been a shift in personal finance. Consumers take advantage of the credit system much more frequently. Although costs have risen everywhere on everything, consumers are now responsible to do more regarding their personal finances. Whereas employers were once responsible for managing pension plans, the tide has turned and it has now become the responsibility of the employee.

individuals need to be equipped with the right tools for success, at least, rudimentary investment skills. As the financial markets continue to become increasingly complex, likewise, individuals need to increase their minimum, basic knowledge of personal finance. Fundamental levels of financial literacy should be reinforced through continuing education comprised of advanced financial literacy theories and skills that complement the complex financial products. Additional research in the field of financial literacy is greatly needed. It allows more in-depth investigations that determine the effects of this type of education on the American population and shows areas that need improvement.

THE PURPOSES

The purposes of this study include: (1) examination of the biblical principles that pertain to personal finance, (2) exploration of the rate of financial literacy possessed by individuals, (3) investigation of any relationships between the financial crisis and financial literacy, (4) examination of the effectiveness and efficiency of the strategies used to promote financial literacy, (5) comparison and contrast of the teaching of financial literacy in conjunction with and without the teaching of behavioral finance, and (6) as a result of the findings, making recommendations for new and improved strategies for continued financial literacy education.

    This study is grounded in the concepts of financial literacy and behavioral finance with concentrations on the rate of financial literacy, the effectiveness of the educational strategies used by public and private educators to promote the teaching of financial literacy, and the emotional reasoning and social factors that explain why individuals manage their personal finance in the particular ways that they do. The study builds upon the related efforts of researchers in the field. The key measures of both the primary and secondary data are financial literacy, numeracy, and cognitive ability. The empirical results will demonstrate any existing correlation between financial literacy and behavioral finance, and highlight any existing need for continued education in financial literacy.

THE SIGNIFICANCE

Although there has been ongoing research in the area of financial literacy, additional research is still essential and of vital importance. This study amplifies the awareness of the need for education in financial literacy. The results of the study re-emphasize the potential economic detriments of financial illiteracy. The study highlights the need for continued education in the field and demonstrates the connection between financial literacy and behavioral finance.

This study builds upon two phenomena in personal finance. The first is that Americans have turned aside from living up to the principles of the American motto and have traded in their trust in God for a false trust in material possessions. The second phenomenon is that millions of Americans lack financial literacy and the discipline to put financial knowledge into action. This study examines the relationship between financial literacy and behavioral finance and illustrates the nationwide need for both.

Chapter 2: Part I

THE TOPIC OF FINANCIAL LITERACY stands out like a beacon in the sea of financial turmoil and signals the attention of organizations, financial counselors, academic economists, consumer advocates, individuals, and families alike. Numerous researchers have undertaken in-depth studies in the field and their conclusions serve as attention-grabbers for the topic. This literature review is based on the Word of God. It begins with a synopsis of the history of the United States of American and demonstrates that men who trusted in God founded the nation on biblical principles. A strong correlation between the nation's motto, pledge of allegiance, coins and currency, and the foundational principles is traced. This study provides an overview of some of the financial literacy programs offered and identifies issues regarding the practicality and successes of some of these programs. This study also compares and contrasts the reports of prior researchers and explains the association or connection between financial literacy and behavioral finance. Lastly, this study discusses the following two catalysts for the financial crisis:

1. Americans have traded their "Trust in God" for a pseudo trust in materialism.
2. Americans have low levels of financial literacy and the ever-increasing complexities of the financial markets are compounding the literacy problem.

AMERICANS HAVE TRADED TRUST IN GOD FOR MATERIALISM

In the seventeenth century, the United States was made up of 13 colonies. Each colony issued its own coins and currency. The coins were inscribed with references to God. The Carolina cent bore the inscription "God preserve Carolina and the Lord's proprietors," New England's coin bore the inscription "God preserve new England," Louisiana's cent bore the inscription "Blessed be the name of the Lord," the Virginia halfpenny bore the inscription "George the Third by the grace of God," and Utah's gold coins bore the inscription "Holiness to the Lord."[19]

On July 4, 1776, the colonies gained independence from Great Britain and became "one nation, under God, indivisible, with liberty and justice for all."[20] Godly men founded the nation of America. The founding Fathers clearly expressed their faith and trust in God through the words of the motto of the United States: "In God We Trust." In 1955, the motto was reinforced when Congress, the House of Representatives, and the Senate unanimously passed a bill that mandated the inscription of the motto on the nation's coins and currency. History records a number of declarations made by the founding fathers, on Jesus, Christianity, and the Bible. Following are a few quotes:

> The general principles on which the fathers achieved independence were the general principles of Christianity. I will avow that I then believed, and now believe, that those general principles of Christianity are as eternal and immutable as the existence and attributes of God. (John Adams).
>
> As to Jesus of Nazareth, my opinion of whom you particularly desire, I think the system of morals and His religion as He left them to us, the best the world ever saw or is likely to see. (Benjamin Franklin).
>
> The doctrines of Jesus are simple, and tend all to the happiness of man .... We all agree in the obligation of the moral principles of Jesus and nowhere will they be found delivered in greater purity than in His discourses . . . . I am a Christian in the only sense in which He wished anyone to be: sincerely attached to His doctrines in preference to all others. (Thomas Jefferson).[21]

As time progressed, the nation experienced a cultural breakdown. As one-by-one each of the founding fathers ended their tenure of leadership,

---

[19] Randy Kamcza. Historical Analysis of the American Civil Liberties Union. "In God We Trust" and the ACLU, 1955 – 1959. Online:
http://www.kon.org/urc/aclu/kamcza.html (18 March 2012).
[20] United States District Court Southern District of West Virginia. *Pledge of Allegiance.* Online: http://www.wvsd.uscourts.gov/outreach/Pledge.htm (18 March 2012).
[21] David Barton, "The Founding Fathers on Jesus, Christianity and the Bible," Wall Builders, May 2008. Online: http://www.wallbuilders.com/libissuesarticles.asp?id=8755 (18 March 2012).

they were replaced by leaders who fostered and encouraged a "materialistic" culture. What was once a God-centered civilization became a dominant self-centered culture that was readily adapted by Americans throughout the nation. Over the years, many Americans exchanged the truth of God for a lie and traded in their Forefather's trust in God the Almighty for a trust in the god of materialism.[22] Even today, many spend their money and time on personal treasures – things that are of paramount value to them and fail to acknowledge negative outcomes (such as financial failure) that can potentially result from trusting in money.[23, 24] The exchange has transcended the centuries. Materialism, as opposed to spiritualism, has become a cultural normalcy that has trickled down through the ages and cuts across socio-economic lines, as individuals become more and more materialistic. People everywhere continue to crave material possessions. They want more and more of it, and never seem to get enough! According to an article in the Washington Times, obsession with materialism is growing among young adults.

> About 80% of American young adults view getting-rich as a top priority in life. Tim Barello, a 24-year-old New Yorker, agrees that his generation has become caught up in wanting more, and more, and more. "To be completely honest," he said, "I don't even appreciate everything I have. I feel empty inside rather often."[25]

The cultural exchange is further observed as individuals with good intentions misuse the lyrics of the American motto. One of the most common ways in which individuals misuse words is by making verbal expressions, knowing in their hearts they truly believe something contrary to that which was spoken. For example, many Americans quote the nation's motto but fail to demonstrate their trust in God. A demonstration

---

[22] Rom. 1.25: "Who changed the truth of God into a lie, and worshipped and served the creature more than the Creator, who is blessed forever. Amen."
[23] Prov. 11.28: "He that trusteth in his riches shall fall."
[24] I Tim. 6.10: "For the love of money is a root of all evil: which whole some coveted after, they have erred from the faith, and pierced themselves through with many sorrows." Luke 12.34: "For where your treasure is, there will your heart be also."
[25] The Washington Times, "Materialism Spikes in a Generation," The Washington Times, 22 January 2007. Online: http://www.washingtontimes.com/news/2007/jan/22/20070122-111119-1982r/print/ (March 20, 2012).

of misused words is explicitly described in the Bible where the Word of God explains that what individuals speak with their mouths and believe in their hearts can be completely contradictory.[26] Individuals misuse words because their personal theologies are contrary to that which was spoken. Although many individuals never verbally express their theologies, the beliefs engrained in their minds steer the courses of their lives. Their beliefs become the focus of all their endeavors and as a result, they align their actions with their beliefs. Many believe they can accomplish all things in their own strength and refuse to believe that all things are accomplished through the power of God.[27]

Like never before in the history of America, there is a turning away from the biblical principles upon which the nation was founded. Whereas the forefathers trusted in and relied upon God, individuals today have strayed away from the Godly trust that once governed the nation and rely on self-trust. They trust in their inner resources such as their minds and emotions, and behave as though money is an individual's ticket to independence from God. They believe they are self-reliant and self-sufficient, and are well able to handle their financial matters according to their personal abilities and plans. Thus, they fail to manage the finances God has placed in their care according to biblical principles. Many who refuse to practice delayed gratification have developed a "want it now" mentality reinforced by self-centered behaviors. The craving and hoarding of possessions has become commonplace. Today's materialistic culture is saturated with diverse forms of consumer financial decisions and activities performed by individuals who lack the knowledge and understanding of God's financial principles. Individuals and families need to return to lifestyles grounded in the biblical principles upon which the nation was founded, and apply God's financial principles to their personal finances. The late President Ronald Regan firmly believed that the nation needed to

---

[26] Isa. 29.13-14: "Wherefore the Lord said, forasmuch as this people draw near me with their mouth, and with their lips do honor me, but have removed their heart far from me, and their fear toward me is taught by the precept of men: Therefore, behold, I will proceed to do a marvelous work among this people, even a marvelous work and a wonder: for the wisdom of their wise men shall perish, and the understanding of their prudent men shall be hid."

[27] Phil. 4.13: "I can do all things through Christ who strengthens me."

revert to trusting in God and live according to Biblical principles. He stated:

> It can be no coincidence that the greatest nation in history just happened to be established on the Christian beliefs and moralities of its founding fathers. It also can be no coincidence that America's decline is lockstep with it's moral decline and it's rejection of it's Judeo-Christian foundation. America's greatness and appeal will not be regained unless it's heritage is restored; The magnificent walls of freedom and liberty . . . will continue to weaken and collapse unless the foundation is repaired and the Founding Fathers original architecture is restored. We can't have it both ways. We can't expect God to protect us in a crisis and just leave Him over there on the shelf in our day-to-day living. America needs God more than God needs America. If we ever forget that we are One Nation Under God, then we will be a Nation gone under. Without God, there is no virtue. Without God, there is a coarsening of the society. And without God, democracy will not and cannot long endure.[28]

The principles of money and finance must be grounded in the Word of God. Before an individual is taught how to handle money, he or she must first be taught where money comes from. It is customary to believe that money is given to individuals in exchange for services rendered. Such an idea or concept causes individuals to believe that they earned the money and are the owners of the money they earned. Individuals should never view money in the sense that they own it instead, they should view it in the sense that they are managers or supervisors who are responsible to manage money according to God's Written Supervisory Procedures as documented in the Bible. The following Scripture verses express that God is the Creator of all things, including money. If he creates all things, then he automatically owns all things, including money.

- In the beginning, God created the heaven and the earth (Gen. 1:1).
- All things were made by him; and without him was not anything made that was made (Jn. 1:3).

---

[28] He That Hath Ears To Hear, Let Him Hear. "America's Christian Heritage: Will our descendants know Biblical moral virtue?" Online: http://www.earstohear.net/heritage/index.html (30 March 2012).

- The earth is the Lord's, and the fullness thereof; the world and they that dwell therein. For he hath founded it upon the seas, and established it upon the floods (Ps. 24:1-2).

The Bible declares that God is the Creator of all things; he established all things and is, therefore, the owner of all things. Nowhere in the Bible is there any mention of God transferring ownership of his possessions to individuals. Instead of transferring ownership to man, God gave man dominion over all the earth to subdue / control / manage all things in the earth (including money).[29] God assigned stewardship to individuals and blesses them by allocating a portion of his finances to them through their employers. God expects his finances to be faithfully managed according to his financial principles as written in his Word. Therefore, his children need to be fully equipped with the Word, financial literacy, and money skills, in order to be thoroughly furnished unto all good works.[30] Comprehension of God's financial principles and possession of the corresponding practical skills can be used as very effective evangelism tools to generate dollars needed to fulfill God's calling to "Go ye therefore, and teach all nations . . ."[31]

Three Biblical financial principles (Creation, Ownership, and Stewardship) are the foundational principles upon which all the other financial principles rest. In order to be successful at personal finance individuals should build their financial structures upon these three basal principles. It is therefore necessary to understand and adhere to these

---

[29] Gen. 1.26 & 28: "And God said, let us make man in our image, after our likeness: and let them have dominion over the fish of the sea, and over the fowl of the air, and over the cattle, and over all the earth, and over every creeping thing that creepeth upon the earth. So God created man in his own image, in the image of God created he him; male and female created he them. And God blessed them, and God said unto them, be fruitful, and multiply, and replenish the earth, and subdue it: and have dominion over the fish of the sea, and over the fowl of the air, and over every living thing that moveth upon the earth."

[30] 2 Tim. 3.17: "All scripture is given by inspiration of God, and is profitable for doctrine, for reproof, for correction, for instruction in righteousness: That the man of God may be perfect, thoroughly furnished unto all good works."

[31] Matt. 28.19: "Go ye therefore, and teach all nations, baptizing them in the name of the Father, and of the Son, and of the Holy Ghost: Teaching them to observe all things whatsoever I have commanded you: and, lo, I am with you always, even unto the end of the world. Amen."

three flagship financial principles as documented in the Word of God. When individuals and families build their financial houses according to biblical financial principles, they position themselves to be greatly blessed by God in every area of their lives, particularly their financial livelihoods. Failure to understand and acknowledge the truths of these principles can become a catalyst for the demise of any financial structure. If the three foundational principles are not understood, all the other principles that build upon them will appear to be silly and meaningless.

THE PRINCIPLE OF CREATION

The Bible contains many scriptures that declare God as the creator of all things. For example, the Bible states:

1. Gen. 1.1: "In the beginning God created the heavens and the earth."
2. Ps. 21.1: "The earth is the Lord's, and the fullness thereof; the world, and they that dwell therein." (The earth refers to the body of rock or soil on which we live and the world refers to human existence.)
3. Jn. 1.3: "All things were made by Him; and without Him was not anything made that was made."

These Scriptures express that God is the source and owner of all things, including all the monies in the world. Nowhere, is it recorded that God transferred ownership of his possessions to his people. According to these principles, individuals do not own anything. Everything belongs to God. However, God transferred stewardship of His possessions to individuals. Therefore, all of the material things that individuals claim they own rightfully belong to God.

THE PRINCIPLE OF OWNERSHIP

The principle of "Ownership" upholds that God owns everything! Individuals do not own anything, not even their bodies. The people of God have been bought with a price. Their bodies are temples of the Holy Spirit. Therefore, everything they do must glorify God, including their handling of the finances he has placed in their care.[32, 33] God instituted work in the first book of the Bible. God assigned man to work as caretakers of the earth and all the things in the earth.[34] Today, many individuals are of the opinion that they work to earn income and, therefore, own the monies they receive as a medium of exchange for their services rendered. They do not understand God's principle of provision, whereby, He provides for them through their employers.[35]

Culture supports the idea that people own the material possessions God has placed in their care. Nowadays, legal documents such as real estate deeds, automobile registrations, bank accounts, and investment certificates are drawn up bearing the names of individuals. These legal instruments allow the bearers to dispose of the properties described in the documents, at will. Such control causes individuals to believe that they rightfully own the articles titled in their names described in the documents. From time to time the holders of legal documents spontaneously repeat the American motto claiming to trust in God. Paradoxically, their actions speak volumes and expressly display their trust in the material possessions they claim ownership of. Although the Bible clearly forbids glorification of anything or anyone other than God himself, many individuals glorify material possessions.[36]

THE PRINCIPLE OF STEWARDSHIP

Stewardship is all-inclusive and encompasses everything an individual does in life. A person's existence is hinged upon stewardship. "A steward acts as an administrator of the affairs and possessions of another and is fully

---

[32] Kenneth Boa. *Stewardship: Your Time, Talent and Treasure*. Online: http://www.kenboa.org/search/?q=stewardship (20 March 2012).

[33] I Cor. 6.19 & 20: "What? Know ye not that your body is the temple of the Holy Ghost which is in you, which ye have of God, and ye are not your own? For ye are bought with a price: therefore glorify God in your body, and in your spirit, which are God's."

[34] Gen. 1.28: "And God blessed them, and God said unto them, be fruitful, and multiply, and replenish the earth, and subdue it: and have dominion over the fish of the sea, and over the fowl of the air, and over every living thing that moveth upon the earth."

[35] Gen. 2.15: "The Lord God took man, and put him into the Garden of Eden to work it and to keep."

[36] Jer. 9.23: "...let not the rich man glory in his riches . . . ."

accountable to his master.[37] The accountability stems from the fact that everything individuals have or that which they have become are gifts from God. Once individuals acknowledge that God owns everything and has allotted portions to each one to be cared for by that person, the next step is to find out how God wants individuals to take care of that which he has given them. God never leaves anyone guessing, he is always specific. He expresses that he wants individuals to "faithfully" manage the things he has given them, according to his procedures as written in his principles.[38] Many individuals ignore God's principles and manage their assets according to their personal philosophies. A popular management style wherein individuals pay themselves first and pay everyone else, including God, after they have paid themselves, is predominantly applied today. The analogy is that if others are paid first, they may not have enough to pay themselves. Especially in these economic times, in order to be good stewards, individuals cannot rely on the manner in which things appear to be. As stewards, they are required to faithfully obey the Word of God, follow biblical principles, and allow God to take care of any financial shortages or other challenges they encounter.

Individuals must be able to identify what things they are accountable for and must therefore have knowledge of the cash and other material possessions that God gave them. God desires that people know their net worth and cash flow.[39] Net worth is calculated by preparing a personal financial statement, also called a balance sheet. A personal financial statement shows a snapshot of an individual's finances at a point in time. Most people fail to create a personal financial statement. By not creating this document individuals are unable to see the true picture of their financial health. Many refrain from setting up personal financial statements because they believe their lifestyles do not warrant setting one up. In other words, they do not possess the items necessary to create such a document. Others ignore setting one up because they choose to continue to exist in a façade atmosphere wherein they remain financially tranquilized and repeatedly tell themselves that they are financially healthy and their

---

[37] Boa.

[38] I Cor. 4.2: "Moreover it is required in stewards, that a man be found faithful."

[39] Prov. 27.23: "Be thou diligent to know the state of thy flocks, and look well to thy herds."

financial lives are okay. As the financial sedation wears off in later years, many individuals are jolted into reality and, once wide awake, realize that they were drowning in debt all along. It is common for individuals and families in this group to owe more than they own, which is called a negative net worth. If they had taken the time to create financial statements, many would have noticed that their finances were upside down. They would have been able to steer away from many of the pitfalls that obstructed and invaded their financial lives and detour in order to improve their future financial condition.

One common mistake individuals make is to use their memory to keep track of financial records. In order to be successful at personal finance, individuals need to maintain their financial records in either electronic or paper formats. Before preparing a personal financial statement, individuals should gather documentation that shows the assets (things they own). They should create a list containing the name and the market value of each asset. Creating a list of the assets owned is helpful as the amounts will later be transferred to the statement of financial condition. Examples of common assets are:

- Cash (in the bank, money market accounts, certificates of deposits, etc.)
- Investments (mutual funds, securities, etc.)
- Home value (market value of the home)
- Automobile value (market value of automobile)
- Personal property value (jewelry, personal items, etc.)
- Value of any other asset owned

The figures should be added up to get the total value of the assets. A list of assets can be seen in Table 1 on the following page:

TABLE 1

LIST OF ASSETS

Checking	$75
Savings	100
IRA	3,000
Mobile Home	45,000
Honda	15,000
Total Assets:	**$63,175**

Next, individuals should examine their liabilities / debts (amounts they owe). Quite similarly to the assets, documentation that shows the liabilities should be gathered and a list containing the name and outstanding balance for each liability should be created. Examples of common liabilities are:

- Mortgage balance
- Loan balance (cars, student, personal)
- Credit card balance(s)

Creating a list of all liabilities is helpful. Quite similarly to the assets, the liabilities will later be transferred to the statement of financial condition. The list will also be used to assist in deciphering the order of paying off debts. The figures should be added up to get the total value of all liabilities and know how much is owed. A list of debts can be seen in Table 2 on the following page:

TABLE 2

LIST OF LIABILITIES

Creditors (Liabilities)	Payoff Amount	Monthly Payments	Due Date	Interest Rate
Mortgage	$35,000	$750	1st	5%
Honda	13,500	400	10th	8%
Visa	4,000	100	8th	23%
Discover	3,500	80	12th	16%
Physicians	850	20	15th	7%
Total Liabilities:	**$56,850**			

The items and amounts from the lists of assets and liabilities should be transferred to the personal financial statement. The difference between the total liabilities and total assets can be a positive or negative number and is called the net worth (how much the individual actually owns or owes). A personal financial statement using the assets and liabilities from Tables 1 and 2 above can be seen in Table 3 on the following page:

TABLE 3

PERSONAL FINANCIAL STATEMENT

Assets		Liabilities	
Checking	$75	Mortgage	$35,000
Savings	100	Honda	13,500
IRA	3,000	VISA	4,000
Mobile Home	45,000	Discover	3,500
Honda	15,000	Physicians	850
		Total Liabilities	$56,850
		Net Worth (NW)	$6,325[40]
Total Assets	$63,175 [41]	Liabilities & NW	$63,175[42]

Note: Later in this report, monthly payments for the amounts in the liability section of this personal financial statement will be calculated and transferred to a spending plan.

Once a personal financial statement has been created, it should be updated each time there is a significant change. For example, it should be revised if there are major additions or deletions to the assets category, or additions or deletions to the liabilities category such as taking on new debt or paying off a credit card. After being able to see from a snapshot how

---

[40] Subtract your total liabilities from your total assets to get your net worth. Your total assets should be the same dollar amount as your total liabilities plus your net worth.
[41] Both sides of a personal financial statement must always be in balance. Total assets MUST always equal total liabilities plus net worth.
[42] A personal financial statement is also called a balance sheet. Both sides of the balance sheet MUST always be in balance or equal to one another.

much is owed, individuals or households should make plans to create a spending plan (budget). The line items in the liabilities category of the personal financial statement will be transferred to the spending plan.

CASH FLOW

A cash flow provides a snapshot of how much money is coming in and how much is going out over a specific period, usually one month. Cash flow is made up of income such as: wages, salary, capital gains from investments, pension/retirement distributions, and expenses or outflows such as: giving, taxes, debt repayment, living expenses, and savings.[43] The cycle of a cash flow can be seen in Chart 1 below.

CHART 1

CASH FLOW

Cash Flow: A process that shows the cycle of income and expenses

There are two types of personal financial statements:

1) The cash flow or income statement, and
2) The balance sheet.

---

[43] Ron Blue. *Master Your Money.* (Chicago: Moody, 2004), 88.

A SPENDING PLAN

A spending plan can be compared to a dessert pie that is portioned and served. God gets the first slice after which the mortgage or rent gets the second and largest slice. The slice for food is smaller and the slices for utilities and other cost-of-living expenses are yet smaller. A slice should always be set aside for the person who manages the pie. Once the slices are all labeled, the spending plan will show precisely how much of an individual's total income is allocated to each area or category of the plan. This is of extreme importance because it is always better for individuals to know where their monies were supposed to go than for them to ask where it went.[44] Analysis of a spending plan allows individuals to take a look at how much money they have, identify where it is going, maximize spending in each category or area of the plan, and make any necessary adjustments to the various categories of the plan. A spending plan is a tool that is vital for successful personal finance.

In today's culture, most individuals will not take the time to develop a spending plan either because they do not understand why they need to have one, do not know how to create one, or believe that working with a spending plan will restrict their spending. For many, the term "spending plan" or "budget" is regarded as a derogatory term that brings pain and grief. They believe that a spending plan will place constraints or restrictions on their finances and they refuse to allow a spending plan to dictate to them or harness their spending habits. Individuals in this category usually spend wildly and wastefully with no accountability and oftentimes, end up over spending. After exhausting their funds, they have no clue where or on what they spent their monies. Many who have worked or attempted to work with a spending plan, started out with good intentions to stick to their plans, then something happened along the way. Unexpected expenses (budget busters) suddenly appear. When this happens, without any type of reservations, many individuals give up working with their spending plans and revert to juggling their finances and

---

[44] Brian Kluth, "Money Matters: Biblical and Financial Insights Into Generosity and Finances," Maximum Generosity. Online: http://www.kluth.org/people/bookchapter.htm (Retrieved 18 March 2012).

worrying about having more "end-of-the-month" than money. Very few individuals attempt to make adjustments to the categories in their spending plan and continue to manage their finances according to a spending plan on a monthly basis

Although there are no specific references to setting up spending plans in the Bible, the principle of setting up a spending plan is scriptural. Firstly, God is a planner.[45] All individuals are made in his likeness and image and should likewise be planners.[46] Secondly, God is a God of order and he desires that individuals live an orderly life. Planning is an essential tool used to bring order to the lifestyles of individuals and families. Without plans, individuals experience chaos. If individuals are not successful at personal finance it is never because they made plans to fail. Instead, it is simply because they failed to plan. Having a working spending plan is one of the most important ingredients for financial stability.

God desires that everyone have knowledge and comprehension of the assets he placed in their care.[47] God requires that individuals plan to give 10% of their income back to him first then use the remainder wisely to take care of their cost-of-living expenses. A preferred spending plan is the 10-10-80 Plan wherein individuals are encouraged to give the first 10% of their income back to God, save 10%, and use the remaining 80% to pay for cost-of-living expenses. This spending plan is grounded in the theory that individuals and households should be able to live comfortably off no more than 80% of their income. Below is a diagram of the 10-10-80 Spending Plan.

---

[45] Jer. 29.11: "For I know the plans I have for you," declares the Lord, "plans to prosper you and not to harm you, plans to give you hope and a future."

[46] Gen. 1.26 & 27: "And God said, Let us make man in our image, after our likeness: and let them have dominion over the fish of the sea, and over the fowl of the air, and over the cattle, and over all the earth, and over every creeping thing that creepeth upon the earth. So God created man in his own image, in the image of God created he him; male and female created he them."

[47] Prov. 27.23: "Be thou diligent to know the state of thy flocks, and look well to thy herds. Commit to the Lord whatever you do and your plans will succeed."

CHART 2

THE 10-10-80 SPENDING PLAN — A PREFERRED SPENDING PLAN

■ **Spending** ■ **Tithes** ■ **Savings**

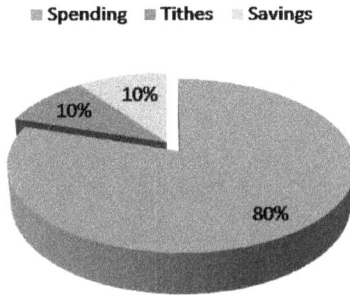

Every home needs a spending plan. However, all the planning in the world will not prove effective and save money unless it is a S.M.A.R.T plan that is:

> ➢ **Specific** –Your plan must precisely fit you. There is no room for generalization. For example, instead of planning to purchase a new computer for about $600.00 in about 6 months, plan to save $25.00 each week and purchase a computer for $600.00 in 6 months ($25.00 each week for 4 weeks equals $100.00 per month times 6 months equals $600.00).

> ➢ **Measurable** – If you save $25.00 each week, starting with the first week of the month, you can measure the accumulation and should have $100.00 at the end of the month. You will take 6 months to reach your goal of $600.00 to purchase your computer.

> ➢ **Attainable** – Your goal must be reachable. Purchasing your computer in 6 months may be possible. However, if the first two items listed above (specific and measurable plans) have not been set, your goal may not be accomplishable.

> ➢ **Realistic** – Do not plan to purchase the computer for $600.00 in 4 weeks by saving $150.00 each week knowing quite well that, due to other obligations, you cannot realistically set aside $150.00 from each paycheck. Instead,

the maximum weekly amount you can afford to set aside is $100.00.

➤ **Time-Bound** – Your goal must have set time to begin and end. In order to accomplish your goal and purchase your computer, you must set a beginning time (month one) and an ending time (month 6).[48]

CREATING A SPENDING PLAN

Before creating a spending plan, it is important to know what percentage of your income should be allocated to the various categories. The following percentages are recommended:

---

[48] University of Northern Iowa. "Create a Budget in 3 Easy Step." Online: http://www.uni.edu/finaid/money-management/create-budget-3-steps (Retrieved 31 March 2012).

TABLE 4

RECOMMENDED PERCENTAGES FOR INCOME ALLOCATION[49]

Number	Category	Recommended Percentage
1	Tithe / Charitable Gifts	10 – 15%
2	Savings	5 – 10%
3	Rent / Mortgage	25 – 35%
4	Utilities	5 – 10%
5	Food	5 – 15%
6	Transportation	10 – 15%
7	Clothing	2 – 3%
8	Medical / Health	5 – 10%
9	Personal	5 – 10%
10	Recreation	5 – 10%
11	Debts	5 – 10%

Following are steps to create a spending plan:

Begin by adding up all income from sources such as paycheck, dividend, interest, pension, social security, rental income, bonus, gifts, child support/alimony, earned income credit, and tax refund. This is your total income. A list of available income can be seen in Table 5, which follows.

---

[49] Source: Data adapted from Dave Ramsey. *Financial Peace University Workbook.* (Brentwood, Tennessee: The Lampo Group, Inc., 2008), 52.

TABLE 5

INCOME

Step 1: List All Available Income

Salary/Wages	$2,000.00
Interest	10.00
Dividends	10.00
Rent (mobile home)	500.00
Other (alimony)	600.00
Total Income per Month	**$3,120.00**

Self-employed individuals, freelancers, and commission-based salespersons, among others, receive income that fluctuates from month to month. Although irregular income makes it more difficult to set up a monthly budget, it is not impossible. In such cases, the average monthly income for the last 12, 6, or 3 months should be used. This means, the individual has to add up 12 months of income and divide the result by 12, or add up 6 months of income and divide the result by 6, or add up 3 months of income and divide the result by 3, to find the average income. Another way to successfully manage a spending plan using irregular income is to base the plan on the lowest irregular income received during a 12-month period. Use of the lowest irregular income crates a safety net during the months when the individual's income is higher.

Next, track all spending for one to three months. Tracking spending is essential. If individuals do not know how much they are spending on the various categories such as food (dining in and out), clothing, and entertainment, they will not be able to establish a plan that reflects their true spending habits. The tracking must be accurate. For example, if an individual account for too much or too little in any area, the spending plan will not accurately mirror that person's cash flow. One good way to track spending is to review bank transactions daily, to capture the transactions that occurred each time the debit card was swiped. Some individuals may need to walk around with a note pad and pen to write down any cash transactions that will not show up in their bank transactions. After 30 to 90 days of tracking spending, an individual may begin to establish a monthly spending plan.[50]

FIXED EXPENSES

There are two types of expenses (fixed and variable). Fixed expenses stay relatively the same each month. Most individuals will have the same items listed in their fixed expenses. Some common items found in most everyone's spending plan are: rent/mortgage, electricity and/or gas, phone, food, and clothing.[51]

TABLE 6

FIXED EXPENSE PANNING

Step 2 (A): List All Fixed Expenses
Fixed expenses do not change over time.

Tithe	$312.00	(10% of total income)
Mortgage/Rent	750.00	(from Table 2 above)
Savings	50.00	(personal decision)
Retirement	100.00	(personal decision)
Automobiles	400.00	(from Table 2 above)
Insurance	50.00	(from Table 7 below)
Debt	200.00	(from Table 2 above)

Total Fixed Expenses: $1,862.00

---

[50] "Build a Basic Budget: The Five-Step Spending Plan." Mountain American Credit Union. Online: https://www.macu.com/pdf/MEB_BasicBudget.pdf (31 March 2012).
[51] See a list of fixed expenses in Table 6 below.

Step 2 (B): List All Periodic Fixed Expenses

Many fixed expenses such as insurance and homeowner's association dues are not paid on a regular monthly basis but must be paid in full at a given time such as quarterly, semiannually, or annually. These types of expenses are called periodic fixed expenses. If these expenses are not planned for, they can become budget busters. Many individuals resort to using borrowed money from credit cards or personal loans to meet these obligations when are due them. If funds are borrowed, the repayment amount creates a new line item in the spending plan and, therefore, the plan needs to be revised. Depending on the tightness of the budget, the additional expense may or may not fit into the spending plan.

In order for the spending plan to properly reflect the periodic fixed expenses, the monthly amounts must be calculated and set aside. To calculate how much should be set aside each month to meet these types of obligations when due, divide the annual payment amount by 12 (months in a year). The answer represents the amount that should be set aside in a savings account each month, in order to have the entire amount when it is due in 3, 6, or 12 months.[52]

TABLE 7

PERIODIC FIXED EXPENSE PLANNING

Type of Expense	Annual Amount	Months	Monthly Amount
Insurance	600.00	÷ 12 =	50.00*

Note: *Auto insurance is $600 annually. Divide by 12 to find out how much should be set aside each month to make the annual payment when due. The monthly payment amount will be added to the fixed expenses in Table 6 above.

---

[52] See Table 7 below.

TABLE 8

VARIABLE EXPENSE PLANNING

Step 2 (C): List Variable Expenses
Variable expenses change from month to month in proportion to activity.

1. Food	$550.00
2. Utilities	$250.00
•Electricity	$150.00
•Gas	$0.00
•Water	$20.00
•Telephone	$60.00
•Cable	$20.00
Total Income per Month	**$800.00**

TABLE 9

INCOME MINUS EXPENSE

Total Income per Month	$3,120.00
Less: Total Expenses	$2,662.00
Fixed $1,862.00	
Variable $800.00	
Unallocated Surplus[53]	**$458.00**

---

[53] Unallocated surplus is the money that is left over after all other obligations have been met. Put it in savings or spend it wisely.

31

SAVINGS

Savings is a self-discipline. A budgeted amount for "Savings" should ALWAYS be included in your Spending Plan. Any positive unallocated surplus at the end of the month should be added to your "Savings" category in order to zero out your budget for the month, and begin anew the following month.

If you are in the "RED" and have a negative surplus at the end of your Monthly Spending Plan, you still need to include a category for "Savings" in your budget, and allocate an amount such as fifty cents ($0.50) to that category. A small amount such as fifty cents will not make or break your budget but will help you to practice a "savings discipline." As you continue to diligently work your way out of the RED by making monthly adjustments, that is, cutting back on your expenses, you will be working towards bringing your budget into balance. Your negative surplus amount will continue to get smaller until it reaches zero and you begin to have a positive surplus amount that is then added to "Savings." The fifty cents that was once allocated to Savings will begin to increase as you continue to develop a habit of self-discipline for savings.

Once the total income and expenses (both fixed and variable) have been tracked, it is time to begin creating the personal spending plan. Following is a blank monthly spending plan in Table 10.

TABLE 10

MONTHLY SPENDING PLAN OVERVIEW

	Budget Amount	Actual Amount	Total Budgeted Amount*	Total Actual Amount**	Difference Surplus / Shortage
Income					
Salary/Wages	$2,000.00	$0,000.00			
Interest	$10.00	$0,000.00			
Dividends	$10.00	$0,000.00			
Mortgage/Rent	$500.00	$0,000.00			
Other	$600.00	$0,000.00			
Total Income			$3,120.00	$0,000.00	$0,000.00
Fixed Expense					
Tithe	$312.00	$0,000.00			
Mortgage/Rent	$750.00	$0,000.00			
Savings	$50.00	$0,000.00			
Retirement	$100.00	$0,000.00			
Automobiles	$400.00	$0,000.00			
Insurance	$50.00	$0,000.00			
Credit Cards	$200.00	$0,000.00			
Total Fixed Expense			$1,862.00	$0,000.00	$0,000.00
Variable Expense					
Food	$550.00	$000.00			
Utilities (Total)	$250.00	$000.00			
• Electricity	$150.00	$000.00			
• Gas	$00.00	$000.00			
• Water	$20.00	$000.00			
• Telephone	$60.00	$000.00			
• Cable	$20.00	$000.00			
Total Variable Expense			$800.00	$000.00	$000.00
Total Expenses (Fixed & Variable)			$2,662.00	$0,000.00	$0,000.00
Income Minus Expense					
Total Income			$3,120.00	$0,000.00	
Less: Total Expenses			$2,662.00	$0,000.00	
Total Income Minus Expenses			$458.00	$0,000.00	
Unallocated Surplus or (Shortage)[54]			$458.00		

* Amounts budgeted for
** Actual amounts (If actual is larger than budgeted, adjust categories.)

---

[54] Use the "actual" amounts to calculate any surplus or shortage, instead of the "budgeted" amounts. A surplus may be used to create a savings account or increase deposits to a retirement account. If there is a shortage, adjustments must be made by decreasing expenses.

Chapter Two: Part II

MOST AMERICANS HAVE LOW LEVELS OF FINANCIAL LITERACY

A NUMBER OF ARTICLES that rate individuals' knowledge and understanding of financial matters were reviewed for this study. Their results have been compared and contrasted. Some of the financial literacy programs offered were examined and the strengths, weaknesses, and success of some of these programs have been highlighted. The association or connection between financial literacy and behavioral finance was also examined.

Among the articles reviewed was a capabilities study performed by the Financial Industry Regulatory Authority (FINRA). This organization is the largest independent securities regulator in the United States. Its primary function is to guard investors against unscrupulous securities transactions. FINRA accomplishes its goal through the establishment of Rules and Guidelines by which its members (service providers) are required to adhere. The FINRA established an Investor Education Foundation (Foundation) in 2003. Through the Foundation, grants earmarked for financial literacy education and research are awarded to businesses. The education and research funded by the grants must be aimed at reaching underserved individuals who possess limited financial literacy. The organization aspires to increase the number of individuals reached each year.

In 2009, the FINRA Foundation collaborated with the United States Department of the Treasury and the President's Advisory Council on Financial Literacy to perform a three-part national study of the rate of financial knowledge possessed by American adults. The sponsoring organizations wanted to understand how individuals save, borrow, and plan for their financial futures. A telephone survey was administered to 1500 participants from among 3 groups (military, adults, and youths). The questions on the survey focused on: (1) making ends meet, (2) planning ahead, (3) managing financial products, and (4) financial knowledge and decision-making. Variables such as behavior and attitude were measured.

The results of the survey suggest that almost 50% of Americans have trouble meeting their monthly expenses. In order to meet their obligations, many overdraw their checking accounts while others borrow from their retirement accounts. A third group of individuals who do not have accounts with overdraft protection or retirement accounts to borrow from default on their payments. According to the results of the survey, the majority of Americans do not have an emergency fund and a large percentage does not have a relationship with a formal financial institutions. The responses gathered suggest that the number one reason many individuals do not use the services of formal financial institutions is because they do not have enough money to bank. It is quite common for individuals who do not engage the services of financial institutions to engage in financial transactions with payday lenders, pawnshops, and rent-to-own businesses. Some of the unbanked individuals take advances on tax returns.

The survey results further suggest that the majority of existing homeowners have fixed mortgages while a small percentage has adjustable rate loans. Regardless of the type of mortgage loan, one in five Americans do not understand mortgage basics and the terms of their contract, and are unable to explain what type of loan they have. This strategically makes them vulnerable and places them in line to experience costly mistakes. The overall findings of the survey highlighted the need for financial literacy education particularly among the underserved. This would empower those in that group with the confidence needed to be successful at personal financial management.[55]

According to Lusardi (2008), due to extremely low levels of financial literacy, many decision-makers do not possess the knowledge and skills necessary to choose wisely.[56] This deficiency has become the Achilles'

---

[55] FINRA Education Investor Foundation, "Financial Capabilities in the United States," National Survey, December 2009. Online: http://www.finrafoundation.org/web/groups/foundation/@foundation/documents/foundati on/p120535.pdf (15 January 2012).

[56] Annamaria Lusardi, "Financial Literacy: An Essential Tool for Informed Consumer Choice?" Dartmouth College, Harvard Business School, and NBER, June 2008. Online: http://www.dartmouth.edu/~alusardi/Papers/Lusardi_Informed_Consumer.pdf (14 July 2011). Individuals were responsible for handling complex day-to-day financial transactions. However, there is evidence that many of these individuals are not capable of making sound financial decisions.

heel for many individuals and families. Such financial weakness can potentially act as a catalyst for financial pitfalls and therefore, is a growing economic and social concern that has captured the attention of governmental agencies, policymakers, financial counselors, academic economists, consumer advocates, individuals, and families alike.

Harnish (2010) supports the idea that many Americans are unable to comprehend basic financial concepts and have difficulty understanding how to efficiently use the services provided by financial institutions. They usually become vulnerable and fall prey to unscrupulous financial services offered by payday lenders and pawnshops. Harnish defines financial literacy as: ". . . the ability to make informed judgments and take effective actions regarding the current and future use and management of money." The lack of financial literacy causes individuals to make costly errors that usually result in record-high levels of debt and low levels of economic security. Many end up experiencing financial hardship caused by poor financial judgments. Although it may not necessarily be that an individual sinned as a result of making a financial mistake, these errors may prevent the individual from accessing the promises of God.[57]

A report published by the Financial Literacy and Education Commission (2010) expresses that "the recent economic crisis has highlighted how essential it is for individuals and families to have the information, education, and tools that they need to make good financial decisions." [58] Without the knowledge of personal financial literacy and money skills, individuals are likely to engage in unscrupulous financial transactions with immoral individuals who customarily take advantage of those with limited financial literacy. This is not God's desire for individuals. God has a divine plan and purpose for everyone. Included in

---

[57] Thomas L. Harnisch, "Boosting Financial Literacy in America: A Role for State Colleges and Universities," Perspectives, American Association of State Colleges and Universities, Fall 2010. Online:
http://www.congressweb.com/aascu/docfiles/AASCU_Perspectives_Boosting_Financial_Literacy.pdf (16 October 2011).

[58] Financial Literacy and Education Commission, "Why and How: Background Report Developing the 2011 National Strategy," November 2010. Online:
http://www.mymoney.gov/sites/default/files/downloads/National%20Startegy%20Backgr ound.pdf (20 July 2011).

God's plan is his desire for individuals to obtain the knowledge, wisdom, and understanding necessary to overcome financial invasion in this world[59]. God wants his people to be examples for the unsaved. Jesus used salt and light as metaphors when He taught about morality and discipleship in the Sermon on the Mount: "You are the salt of the earth. But if the salt loses its saltiness, how can it be made salty again? You are the light of the world . . . let your light shine before others, that they may see your good deeds and glorify your Father in heaven (Matt. 5.13-16).

Salt is used in a many ways for a number of reasons. Salt is used as a preservative in foods such as fish or meat to prevent spoilage. Just as salt preserves foods, Christians are expected to teach others how to preserve or guard against financial pitfalls. As God's people lead by example and show others how to manage their finances according to his directives, they will be the salt that preserves others. However, if Christians lack training in this area, how can they teach something they do not understand? Christians should lead by example.

Salt is used as a seasoning to enhance and bring out the flavor in foods. Likewise, the body of Christ is expected to exemplify in everything they do, particularly in the handling of money. Christians should teach others how to bring out God's flavor (or will) for the handling of personal finances. God wills that everyone prosper in body (including health and finances) and soul.[60] Prosperity means more than just getting by. When Christians live lifestyles that demonstrate prosperity through Godly handling of their finances, they metaphorically become the seasoning that enhances and brings out God's flavor in personal financial management.

Salt is used as a purifying agent. Traditionally, the umbilical cord by which a baby receives all its nourishment was cut and knotted at birth. In order to cleanse/purify the baby's skin, the infant was washed with a mixture of salt and water to create firmness in the skin and cause it to contract or shrink, then wrapped in swathing cloth to give firmness to the muscles until they were strong enough to support the body. As purifying agents, Christians are called upon to bring the message of Christ to a

---

[59] Prov. 4.5-7: "Get wisdom . . . and with all thy getting get understanding."
[60] 3 John 1.2: "Beloved, I wish above all things that thou mayest prosper and be in health, even as thy soul prospereth."

world in need of purification. The handling of money is one of the best places to start with purification. Christians should not deal underhandedly and engage in fraudulent business activities. When God's people adhere to his Word, particularly his financial principles, they act as purifying agents in this world.[61]

In a report published by Semommung (2011), he mentions that there is a crucial need for financial literacy. He believes that having an understanding of personal finance will help households to avoid many of the financial struggles and pitfalls they encounter on a daily basis. He urges individuals and families to take this matter seriously as everyone, everywhere, no matter what they do, needs money to take care of daily necessities. Americans are not financially literate and are unable to properly manage their finances. They do not understand the characteristics of the daily financial activities in which they engage. Many find it difficult to create stable lifestyles and sound futures. Man's greatest enemy nowadays is said to be the lack of financial education.[62]

Despite the fact that most individuals must deal with money every day primarily to take care of their physical needs such as housing, food and clothing, a large number do not invest any time or effort to find out about money. On an average, many individuals spend eight hours working for money each day, but spend no time learning how money works. The lack of financial literacy creates an atmosphere wherein individuals and households engage in financial activities that produce negative results with negative consequences and many end up leading impoverished lives. Education in personal finance should be upheld by everyone as "an important personal endeavor worth undertaking for the good of all."[63]

Most individuals desire economic stability and security for themselves, their families, and future generations. Needless to say, most

---

[61] Adam Clarke. "Commentary on the Bible." Online: http://www.sacred-texts.com/bib/cmt/clarke/eze016.htm. "On the day you were born your cord was not cut, nor were you washed with water to make you clean, nor were you rubbed with salt or wrapped in cloths" (Ezek. 16.4).

[62] Ben Semommung, "Discover the Power of Financial Education!" The Ultimate Allowance, 11 February 2011. Online: http://ultimateallowancebook.com/blog/?p=297 (7 July 2012). "One of mankind's greatest enemies (was) found to be the lack of education in financial literacy."

[63] Ibid.

individuals in the poorer classes of people live in high-risk neighborhoods. Some get by solely on subsidized dollars. In order to satisfy daily necessities, deal with emergencies, grab hold of opportunities that presented themselves, and plan for the future, proper management of the small amounts of finances they receive is vital. The accumulation of assets, which is primarily done by savings, is of major importance. Many of those in this group are either unbanked or under-banked and pay high costs for expensive informal services. Individuals in this group need access to formal financial services along with the knowledge of how to use the services. "Financial education training will equip those in this class with the knowledge, skills and attitudes to better manage their money and to make informed choices when faced with different financial options."[64]

Many individuals in the lower income bracket face a myriad of financial challenges from cash flow pressures. These common, persistent, and often urgent day-to-day challenges make long-term planning impossible for many. Future plans are often of a short-term nature and correspond to immediate needs, seasonal expenses, or tuition. It is not uncommon to find that women are the ones who bear the responsibility of managing the household's cash. Many women find this job to be extremely difficult, particularly because they do not have back-up or reserved resources and, furthermore, they possess limited financial literacy and are therefore unable to make informed decisions.

Although many organizations now offer education in financial literacy, individuals who received training are still challenged by the array of new and improved financial products from which they must choose. Many do not fully understand how the financial products work and are unable to make the right decisions. Many unbanked individuals who do not have access to banking services obtain financial assistance from families, friends, moneylenders, and pawnshops, among other informal systems. Many of the informal systems offer expensive, insecure, inefficient, and inadequate services. Although costly and a deterrent of savings, the

---

[64] M. Cohen, E. McGuiness, J. Sebstad and K. Stack, "Financial Education: From Poverty to Prosperity," Market Research for Financial Education, A Working Paper, 2006, 3. Online: http://microfinanceopportunities.org/docs/Market_Research_for_Financial_Education.pdf (25 March 2012).

informal services played a vital role in the lives and money management systems of many individuals and families. In order to reduce spending, countless adjustments are made. For example, many cut back on basic expenditures such as food, clothing, education, and health care. Some change their diets, and reduce the number of meals consumed per day. If there is no financial relief, some relocate to less expensive dwelling units.

Financial literacy, described as an essential for successful personal finance, is found at the base of thriving individuals, families, and communities. On the contrary, financial illiteracy directly attacks the well-being of impoverished individuals. There are millions of Americans who do not understand the fundamentals of basic financial principles and lack basic numeracy skills. This deficiency is identified as a major deterrent to the demand for financial products and services. Opening and maintaining saving and checking accounts is one of the primary ways in which the underserved households participate in formal financial services. When required to work with financial products such as bank accounts, individuals with limited financial knowledge experience feelings of discomfort. If individuals experience discomfort or feel insecure when they use a particular financial product or service, they will refrain from using that product or service. Not having the skills necessary to work with rudimentary products leave many individuals no choice but to engage in financial transactions that result in sizeable interest payments and fees.[65] Financial literacy is described as an economic stimulus designed to improve the economy. The rate of financial literacy has a direct relationship with the rate of the economy. Any increase in the rate of financial literacy will trigger a corresponding increase in the rate of the economy. An increase in the rate of financial literacy among those without savings and checking accounts will increase the demand for those products.

Every 3 years, the Federal Reserve performs a Survey of Consumer Finances (a study of 4,500 households). The results of the study help the government to understand many of the financial issues that

---

[65] Shaw Cole, Thomas Sampson, and Bilah Zia. "Prices or Knowledge? What Drives Demand for Financial Services in Emerging Markets?" A Working Paper, 2010. Online: http://www.hbs.edu/research/pdf/09-117.pdf (2 August 2011).

underprivileged individuals face. Results of the study suggest that families in the lower-income bracket spend approximately $500 each year for the services of alternative providers such as pawnshops and pay-day-lenders. Similar services would cost about $60 at a traditional banking institution. Needless-to-say, lower-income families unnecessarily lose a small fortune as a result of not using mainstream banking. The monies lost in excessive interests and fees could have been deposited to a demand account and saved for a rainy day.[66] The results of the 2010 study are displayed on Chart 3 below.

---

[66] Family Services Center. Pawnshop loans were found to be approximately 15 times more expensive than loans from a traditional banking institution.

CHART 3

FEDERAL RESERVE SURVEY OF CONSUMER FINANCES

Respondents were asked some questions about their usage of checking accounts. When asked the reason they failed to maintain a checking account:

- 28.4% did not write enough checks to make it worthwhile
- 18.5% did not like dealing with banks
- 7% did not know how to manage or balance a checking account
- 1% indicated that the locations and/or hours of operation was inconvenient

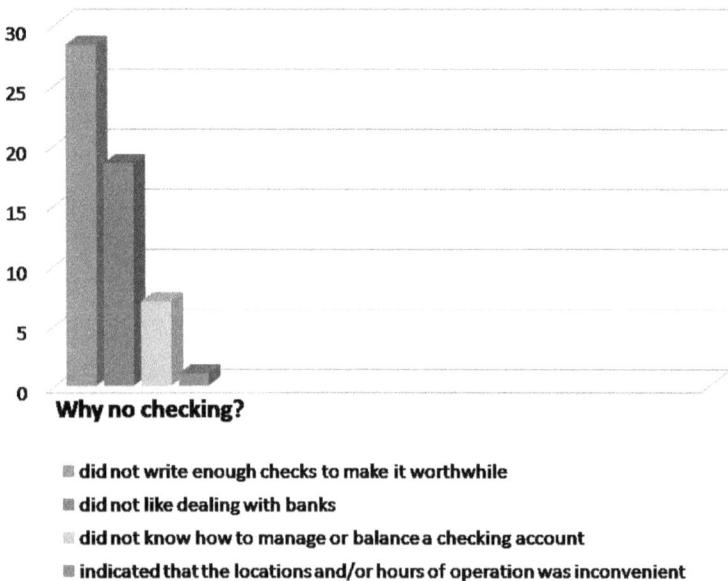

Why no checking?

- did not write enough checks to make it worthwhile
- did not like dealing with banks
- did not know how to manage or balance a checking account
- indicated that the locations and/or hours of operation was inconvenient

Source: Data adapted from Family Service Center, 2004, online at http://www.fsc-hsv.org/moneymgt-finliteracy.htm.

Note: Percentages are based on 118.6 million U.S. households. Percentages do not always sum to 100 because of the rounding of household weights to represent the population totals. These households are banked, but there is not enough information to determine if they are under-banked.

The United States Bureau of Labor Statistics (BLS) conducts a monthly Current Population Survey (CPS). Each month, a sample consisting of about 54,000 households made up of individuals 15 years and older are interviewed through computer-assisted personal and telephone interviewing. Social, economic and geographic data such as employment, unemployment, earnings and other characteristics of the general labor force, plus demographic characteristics such as age, sex, race, marital status and education are collected and analyzed. The data represents the 118.6 million American households. Some of the data is broken down into segments that represent various subgroups.

A survey was performed in 2009. The aim was to collect data on unbanked and under-banked households. The results of the survey suggest that, as an alternative to using the services of federally insured institutions, many households resort to using expensive financial service providers like payday lenders and check advance loans. Aside from paying more for basic financial transactions, households in this group are also more susceptible to identity theft. Oftentimes, borrowers lack sufficient funds to pay off the loan. In such instances, they are allowed to pay a new transaction fee and extend the terms of the loan. What started off as a short-term high-interest loan quickly escalates to a long-term high-interest one. Extension of the loan can go on endlessly and before long, the cost of the loan can exceed the actual loan amount by a wide margin.

About 86% of the 54,000 participants in the sample (about 47,000 individuals) took part in the 2009 survey. Among the key findings are the following:

- an estimated 70.3% of U.S. households approximately 83 million) are banked,
- an estimated 7.7% of U.S. households (approximately 9 million) are unbanked,
- an estimated 17.9% of U.S. households (approximately 21 million) are under-banked,
- an estimated 25.6% of U.S. households (approximately 30 million) are either unbanked or under-banked, and

- an estimated 4.1% of U.S. households (approximately 5 million) are believed to be banked; however, their use of the mainstream banking system cannot be determined and, therefore, many in this category are assumed to be under-banked.[67]

CHART 4

BANKING STATUS OF U.S. HOUSEHOLDS

This chart demonstrates the key overall findings of FDIC National Survey of Unbanked and Under-banked Households. The goal of the survey is to ensure that all households have access to basic, safe, and affordable banking services offered by federally insured financial institutions.

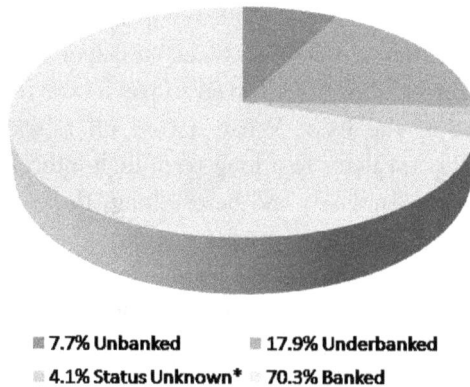

- 7.7% Unbanked
- 17.9% Underbanked
- 4.1% Status Unknown*
- 70.3% Banked

Source: Data adapted from the 2009 FDIC National Survey of Unbanked and Under-banked Households.

Note: Percentages are based on 118.6 million U.S. households. Percentages do not sum to 100 because of the rounding of household weights to represent the population totals.

* These households (4.1%) are banked, but there is not enough information to determine if they are under-banked.

[67] See Chart 4 below.

Another noteworthy point in the findings of the 2009 CPS survey performed by BLS is the suggestion that households with no college education are in the lead position for not having a relationship with a federally insured financial institution. Many individuals in this group were asked to give the reasons they did not use the services of a banking institution. The most common response given was that those in this category do not have enough money to bank. They are described as households in the lower income bracket making less than $25,000 annually. The second most popular answer was that many did not understand how the banking system worked. Of the overall unbanked segment of households, a considerable portion believes that they will have no future need to open a bank account. However, a small percentage believes that they are very likely to open a bank account in the future.[68]

The survey results show that unbanked households use money orders, payday lenders, pawnshops, and check cashing institutions for their day-to-day financial transactions. Households in this group are usually not financially literate and therefore do not understand the basics of the banking system. Due to such deficiency, members of these households will feel intimidated if they are compelled to use banking products such as demand accounts, without first learning how these products work.[69] In an attempt to bridge the unbanked and under-banked gap, the United States and Federal Governments passed legislations regarding "lifeline" banking and provided incentives to retail banks that operated in underserved areas.[70]

In order to accelerate the promotion of financial literacy programs the government of the United States established the President's Advisory Council on Financial Literacy ("PACFL"), in 2008. The primary role of the PACFL is to promote programs aimed at improving financial literacy with the expectation that increased financial literacy will in turn increase the

---

[68] FDIC National Survey of Unbanked and Underbanked Households. "Executive Summary," December 2009. Online:
http://www.fdic.gov/householdsurvey/executive_summary.pdf (15 August 2011).
[69] Ibid.
[70] Cole, et al. Laws were established to govern lifeline banking. Accordingly, state-chartered banks were mandated to offer low-cost checking accounts ($3.00 per month) that required no minimum balance, to accounts that were opened with very small deposit.

demand for financial products and services. The PACFL supports many low-cost initiatives that assist under-banked and unbanked households with financial decision-making. The organization believes that financial literacy education should become a mandatory part of the curriculum for all schools, from Pre-K through 12. Any school that does not offer financial literacy in their curricula is encouraged to adopt the "Money Math: Lessons for Life" curriculum, created by the United States Treasury and endorsed by the PACFL. The curriculum demonstrates ways in which the government is able to collaborate with organizations to produce teaching materials designed to make teaching financial literacy easier for the educator and more comprehendible for the student.[71]

The PACFL believes that today's education system is not equipped with teachers who are trained to teach the students how money works, therefore, the system cannot produce graduates who are able to successfully manage their finances. On an average, first year college students carry credit card balances of $1301.00. By their senior year, the debt increases to $2,623. Overall, more than 52% of college students accumulate more than $5000.00 in credit card debt while in school, and 33% rack up more than $10,000 prior to graduation. Many students are experiencing financial difficulties and display no inclinations to save money. Credit card and student loan debt are two of the major prohibiting factors for opening and maintaining savings account. Concerns for the rising debt levels among students have triggered the Council's recommendation that the youth are urgently in need of debt management education. Most of the students from K-12 will graduate without having any formal classroom education in financial literacy. For this reason, financial literacy needs to be incorporated in the curriculum of all schools across the nation and should become a mandated subject for every child from K-12. These lessons should continue on through college.[72]

When polled about their rate of financial literacy, results show that Americans overestimate their rate of financial knowledge. Although many

---

[71] President's Advisory Council on Financial Literacy, "2008 Annual Report to the President," The Department of the Treasury, 22 January 2008, 1 & 15. Online: http://www.financialeducationbook.com/making-bank-book/wp-content/uploads/2011/03/PACFL_ANNUAL_REPORT_1_16_09.pdf (5 July 2011).
[72] Ibid., 12-15.

profess to be financially literate, they fail to perform proper analysis of financial information and appear overwhelmed with the plethora of information that exists on the subject. The volume of information is so gigantic, many do not know where to begin their analyses and end up taking no action regarding personal financial management. To compound the problem, due to the extremely private nature of personal finance, individuals who are challenged by personal finance refrain from speaking out and asking for help. The desire for privacy and the lack of trust in other people cause many to become financial introverts who fail to seek the assistance of outside professionals. As their financial situations worsen, as is usually the case, it becomes even more of a private matter.[73]

The PACFL recommends that tools necessary to perform self-assessments of personal financial knowledge and overall financial health are made accessible on the internet and also in paper formats, to assist households in the evaluation of their financial knowledge and health. The self-assessment instruments should be made up of a series of ten questions that addressed basic skills such as:

1. Budgeting
2. Evaluation of the affordability of a purchase
3. Establishment and maintenance of an emergency fund
4. Understanding the FICO (Fair Isaac Company) score and knowing how credit works
5. Understanding credit cards
6. Understanding savings and compound interest
7. Understanding the basics of a mortgage transaction
8. Knowing how much insurance is needed and be familiar with the various insurance products
9. Knowing and understanding the benefit programs available through employers or other member organizations
10. Understanding the basic retirement vehicles, the need for retirement plans, and how they work

---

[73] Ibid., 23.

Individuals who score low on their self-assessment tests will be directed to a database that offers aggressive self-tutoring programs that, once established, will be displayed on a public website where participants will be able to access them. Participants will be able to monitor their scores and improvements over time, as they continue to access and work with the self-tutoring programs.[74]

Financial literacy is regarded as a lifelong endeavor. Therefore, it is never too early to begin learning about money. In order for children to become successful personal financial managers in adulthood, it is necessary for the basic financial literacy skills, also called building blocks of development and self-sufficiency, to be embedded in their lives at an early age. Lessons on the terminologies, skills, and behaviors of financial literacy must be an ongoing process throughout life, beginning at a very early age. When children are taught financial lessons at an early age, they develop the foundation needed to understand financial concepts.[75]

The Jump$tart Coalition for Personal Financial Literacy (J$CPFL) is a national coalition of organizations dedicated to improving the financial literacy of youths from K-12. The coalition functions as a voice for the youth. The Coalition also performs research studies, initiates educational programs for the youth, and provides the various resources required to make the programs successful. The coalition's aim is to equip children with the tools necessary to become adults who are successful at personal financial management. The J$CPFL believes that high school graduates should be held responsible for their personal financial well-being and should be expected to know how to process financial information, set goals, and make plans to realize the goals that were set. A high school graduate should know how to earn money and how to properly manage the monies that he or she earns to meet financial obligations, save, and invest. In order to accomplish this, the J$CPEL created and maintains the "National Standards in K-12 Personal Finance Education."[76]

---

[74] Ibid., 42-43.

[75] Ibid., 19.

[76] Jump$tart Coalition for Personal Financial Literacy, "National Standards in K-12 Personal Finance Education," 2007, 3rd Edition, 1 & 2. Online: *http://www.jumpstart.org/assets/files/standard_book-ALL.pdf* (5 August 2011).

Another promoter of financial literacy for the youths is Junior Achievement (JA). This organization believes that financial literacy is of critical importance and recommends that the subject is mandated as a requisite for students of all ages, to equip them with "the tools and knowledge they need to plan for their future, make smart academic and economic choices," and survive in complex economies. JA leads by example. With the assistance of classroom volunteers, JA empowers young people nationwide from K-12 with the financial literacy skills necessary to reach their potentials.[77]

Organizations and learning institutions are not solely responsibility for educating children in financial literacy. Each generation bears the responsibility of passing on the Word of God, including His financial principles, to the next generation.[78] God does not begin anew with each generation. He charged Israel with training up their children according to biblical principles.[79] Therefore, parents are responsible for teaching their children many principles, including principles of financial literacy, during their growing-up years. When the child is ready for school, financial literacy training should continue throughout the child's school years. Children need more than verbal instructions. Instead of merely instructing children on what to do, parents must lead by example and show children what to do.[80] Before parents can teach children how to manage money, they must first be able to successfully manage their own financial affairs. However, a large number of parents are not financially literate and therefore, are unable to teach that which they do not know. Parents cannot successfully teach principles with which they are not familiar.

---

[77] Junior Achievement, "Teens and Careers Survey," Executive Summary, 2010. Online: http://www.ja.org/ (31 July 2012).

[78] Prov. 6.22: "Train up a child in the way he should go, even when he is old, he will not depart from it."

[79] Deut. 6.6 & 7: "These commandments that I give you today are to be on your hearts. Impress them on your children. Talk about them when you sit at home and when you walk along the road, when you lie down and when you get up."

[80] I Pet. 5.3: "Neither as being lords over [God's] heritage, but being ensamples to the flock."

Oftentimes, parents feel that they did not do a good job of teaching their children about money.[81]

Parents should actively involve children in everyday financial transactions that include the following four principles of money management: earning, saving, spending, and giving. The best way to create a society of financially literate adults is to harness bad money habits by stepping in front of those bad traits before they begin to rear their ugly heads up, and teach basic money skills to children at an early age. Therefore, parents needed to pass their financial values on to their children. Following is a three-step formula for teaching children about money:

1) In the case of two-parent households, both parents should discuss the issue before it is brought to the child's attention.
2) Parents should go back into time and try to recall what their financial concerns were at the time they were the age of the child who is being tutored.
3) Open discussions should be held during which the child should be allowed to express his or her opinions about money.[82]

Parents should begin teaching their children money lessons prior to the time the children reach school age and certainly before they reach teenage years. A good place to start is when the children begin to ask their parents to buy them stuff. Children should be taught that things are not free. If parents begin teaching their children about money when they begin to recognize money, the children will develop money habits that are both short-term and long-term. In the near-term children will learn how to make smart money decisions to spend wisely and save, and will acquire the concept of delayed gratification while they saved to purchase larger things. In the long-term children will learn to refrain from accumulating debt and

---

[81] Andrew Lendnal, *Gold Start: Teaching Your Child About Money.* (New Zealand Exisle Publishing Limited, 2011) 7.

[82] Ibid., 13. Individuals have different feelings and opinions about money based on childhood experiences, and family values, and beliefs. For those reasons, parents are required to discuss their opinions beforehand and establish a unified approach prior to the time they held discussions with their children.

will also learn the basic steps in planning for their financial future by investing. Children should be taught how to treat their income similarly to the way they treated their allowance. "The benefits of teaching children good money habits (will) make it well worth the effort. Children who (are not) taught these lessons (will) suffer the consequences for a lifetime." [83]

Children learn about money from their parents primarily through observation. They listen to their parents talk about money (directly or indirectly) and keenly watch the ways in which their parents spend money. If parents spend all the money they earn – sometimes before they earn it – that makes it impossible for them to teach their children to limit their resources, spend according to a spending plan, and save a portion of their earnings. On the contrary, if parents hoard their earnings and do not spend, children will not be able to see money as a tool and will regard money as a goal.

One of the best ways to start educating children on handling money is to give them an allowance so that they can begin to practice the money skills taught. With the guidance of their parents, they should be allowed to make financial decisions on what to do with their allowance. Parents should decide on giving children an allowance. Parents may decide to make loans to children. Be sure to charge them interest. Having to pay loans back with interest should encourage children to stay away from loans when they are older. Another important action-step is to teach children how to make good financial decisions. Children can use actual money from their allowance. With the guidance of their parents, they should choose how to spend the money. The following three activities below will help pre-teens to understand the value of money:

1) Save for short-term goals
2) Make deposits (not withdrawals) to a demand account at a local financial institution
3) Comparison-shop and wait for sales

---

[83] Ibid., 13. Parents should "start early to raise financially responsible adults. The sooner (they start), the less scary it (would) be."

It is quite common to find young adults who are not trained in financial literacy drowning in unmanageable credit card debt, car payments, and student loans. They do not know much about money but enjoy spending it. A vivid picture is painted of students who quickly sign up for their first credit card. Much too quickly, they max it out and sign up for others. This pattern repeats itself for a while. Not long thereafter, many of these students apply for student loans and use the borrowed funds to pay off their credit cards. By the time they graduate from college, they are $10,000 or $20,000 in the hole. A few years later, their debt climbs to $30,000. Surprisingly, they lose absolutely no sleep over their load of debt. As they mature, they become accustomed to living with debt and no savings. This happens because of the culture in which they live – a culture wherein financial illiteracy has become the norm of the day and overspending is thought to be a simple mistake. To compound the matter, the culture encompasses an ever-changing economy.

Across the nation, a large number of government officials, educators and organizations have turned up the volume on the need for financial literacy education for individuals of all ages. The Government Accountability Office (GAO) strongly promotes the teachings of such skills. The agency performs research studies for Congressional committees and subcommittees. Its main responsibility is to investigate how the government spends taxpayers' dollars, and recommend more efficient, effective, ethical, and equitable ways of spending. The results of studies performed by the GAO lead to the creation of laws and acts enforced by the government.

The GAO performed a study to measure the rate of financial literacy among Americans. In their report of the findings, the GAO expressed that the continuum of economic changes have created a greater need to empower Americans with the right tools necessary for successful personal finance. A survey was performed. According to the results, most individuals consider themselves to be "good at dealing with day-to-day financial matters." [84] Quite contradictorily, further results show that many

---

[84] Government Accountability Office. "Financial Literacy: The Federal Government's Role in Empowering Americans to Make Sound Financial Choices," 12 April 2011. Online: http://www.gao.gov/new.items/d11504t.pdf (1 August 2011).

do not understand basic financial concepts. Due to the lack of comprehension in financial matters, 25% of households are unbanked and rely on the use of non-bank, high-cost financial products and services of check-cashing businesses and payday lenders. When compared to the services of formal financial institutions, these products and services offer less favorable terms and conditions. Overall, the results of the study suggest that there is a nationwide low rate of financial literacy among Americans. This raises additional concerns because although the rate of financial literacy is extremely low individuals have been handed the responsibility of planning for retirement and managing their retirement assets.

A study was undertaken by Lusardi and Mitchell (2006), to test the confidence of Americans age 50+ regarding:

1) the formulas used to figure out the amount of money needed for retirement,
2) how they plan to accumulate the amount needed for retirement, and
3) how they manage their retirement accounts.

The results of surveys suggest that less than 33% of individuals try to devise a retirement plan and more than 80% of all individuals feel they cannot successfully plan for retirement. Individuals who made financial plans displayed financial knowledge. It can, therefore, be inferred that financial knowledge and financial planning are interrelated.[85]

The following 3 questions were included in the survey:

1) Suppose you had $100 in a savings account and the interest rate was 2% per year. After five years, how much do you think you would have in the account if you left the money to grow: more than $102, exactly $102, less than $102?

2) Imagine that the interest rate on your savings account was 1% per year and inflation was 2% per year. After 1 year, would you be

---

[85] Lusardi, 1.

able to buy more than, exactly the same as, or less than today with the money in this account?

3) Do you think that the following statement is true or false: Buying a single company stock usually provides a safer return than a stock mutual fund?

The first 2 questions assessed the participants' knowledge of financial concepts and competency with basic numeracy skill. The last question evaluated the respondents' knowledge of risk diversification. The results of the study suggest an overall low level of financial literacy among older individuals. One-half of the respondents correctly answered the first 2 questions and only one-third of the respondents were able to answer all 3 questions correctly.[86] The overall results of the survey suggested that most individuals cannot perform simple economic calculations and lack knowledge of basic financial concepts.[87]

A survey was administered to early baby boomers who turned 51- to 56-years-old in 2004. Individuals in this group are regarded as being close to the end of their wealth-accumulation stage and are therefore prime subjects for surveys of this nature. The following two questions were included in the survey:

1) If the chance of getting a disease is 10 percent, how many people out of 1,000 are expected to get the disease?

2) If 5 people all have the winning number in the lottery and the prize is 2 million dollars, how much will each of them get?

All respondents who answered either one of these first two questions correctly were then asked the following question:

---

[86] Ibid., 4-5. Most individuals lacked knowledge in basic financial concepts such as working with compound interest, knowing the difference between nominal versus real numbers, and the basics of risk diversification when dealing with investments. Knowledge of the more complex concepts such as the basics of mutual funds, stocks, and bonds was less likely to be found among everyday individuals.
[87] Ibid., 8.

4) Let's say you have 200 dollars in a savings account. The account earns 10% interest per year. How much would you have in the account at the end of two years?

The results of the baby boomer survey are displayed in Table 10 below.

TABLE 11

FINANCIAL LITERACY AMONG EARLY BABY BOOMERS

The Table below shows the rate of financial literacy among baby boomers who turned 51 to 56-years-old in 2004. The responses to the three questions above are disclosed in the table.

Question Type	Correct %	Incorrect %	Do Not Know %
Question # 1	83.5	13.2	2.8
Percentage Calculation			
Question # 2	55.9	34.4	8.7
Lottery Division			
Question # 3 Compound Interest*	17.8	78.5	3.2

Source: Data adapted from Lusardi (2008), 25.

Percentages may not sum to 100 due to a few respondents who refused to answer the questions.

*This question was conditional. It was contingent on the participants responding to either question # 1 or question # 2 correctly.

The overall results of the baby boomers survey suggest that financial knowledge and numeracy skills are extremely low among adults. Only slightly more than half (55%) of individuals are able to divide two million dollars by five. The majority of individuals are unable to understand the science of compound interest. Only 18% of individuals are able to correctly compute compound interest. According to the results of the survey, "of those who got the interest question wrong, 43% undertook a simple interest calculation."[88]

The focus of the surveys shifted to planning for the future including saving and investing. A group of college graduates were surveyed. The focus of the survey was to test the participants' understanding of the relationship between investment risk and return. The results of the survey suggest that advance knowledge of financial literacy is not widespread even among individuals with higher education.[89] The results of numerous other surveys on topics including but not limited to economics, money, interest rates, finance, inflation, credit, savings, mortgages, and general financial management were examined. The results demonstrated that adults scored Cs while high school students scored Ds and Fs.

Aside from being widespread, financial illiteracy is acute among particular demographic groups and declines sharply with age. Notwithstanding, many seniors are required to be responsible for managing their finances and oftentimes, they unknowingly engage in financial scams with unscrupulous individuals who prey upon them. For this reason, this decline is of major concern. Chart 3 on the following page shows the decline by age group.[90]

---

[88] Ibid., 7.

[89] Ibid., 10. Where traces of limited financial literacy were evident, there rose concerns as to whether the respondents actually comprehend the question. To investigate such concerns, two groups were chosen. Simple question were reworded. The same question with different words was asked to each group. For example, the first group was asked if bonds were normally riskier than stocks. The second group was asked if stocks were normally riskier than bonds. Results showed that the wording of that simple question did not really matter. A complex question was asked to both groups. The first group was asked: "What would happen to bond prices if interest rates fell?" The second group was asked: "What would happen to bond prices if interest rate roses?" Most of the responses to the question appeared to have been "guess" answers. Therefore, it was noted that the wording of this complex question did matter to the respondents.

[90] Ibid., 11. Financial literacy declines strongly with age. Since individuals are required to make financial decisions until late in life, this is an important finding. There are concerns regarding the elderly and predatory financial transactions.

CHART 5

FINANCIAL LITERACY BY AGE

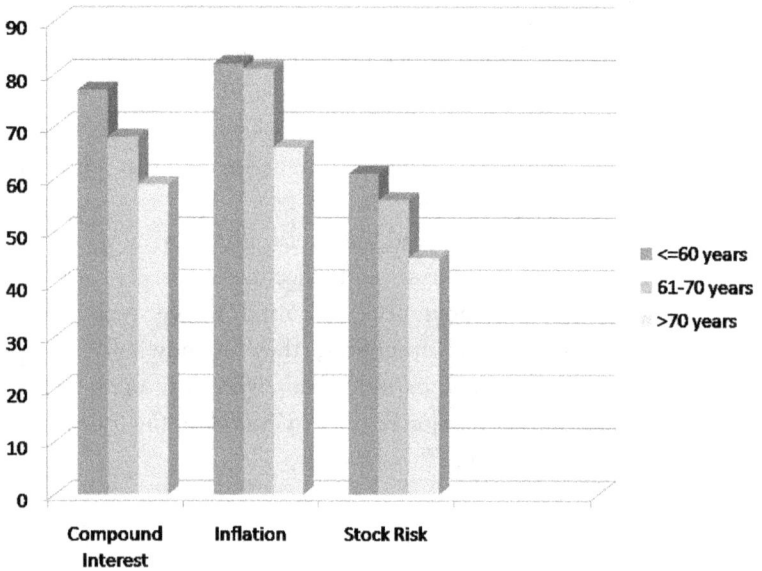

Legend:
- ■ <=60 years
- ▨ 61-70 years
- ▧ >70 years

X-axis: Compound Interest, Inflation, Stock Risk

Source: Data adapted from Lusardi (2008), 28.

Note: financial literacy declines strongly with age. This is an important finding as individuals are required to make financial decisions until late in life and there is great concern about the elderly and incidences of financial scams with individuals who prey upon the elderly.

It is quite common to find that most individuals are unable to articulate the numbers on their real estate disclosures after closing on their loans. Americans of all ages tend to be ignorant when it comes to money matters. Ignorance is not always bliss. What individuals do not know can be harmful. Americans do not understand the basics of money matters as well as they should. Such financial illiteracy, experts believe, helped to set the stage for the existing financial crisis. For example, an article published in the June 2005 Economist states that the boom in the price of real estate was driven by the following two common denominators:

1) Historically low interest rates
2) Consumers' desire for maximum returns on their investments

The low interest rates attracted borrowers and influenced them to borrow more money. Also, many individuals and families lost confidence in the stock market that plummeted a couple of years earlier, and were looking for an investment that would yield maximum returns.[91] During the 2005 housing boom, the low interest rates made purchasing a home cheaper and somewhat justified the steep increase in prices. Although borrowers did not fully understand the characteristics of a real estate transaction, investment in real estate appeared to be extremely attractive and seemed like the way to go. The homeownership rate rose rapidly as can be seen in Chart 6 below.

---

[91] The Economist, "The Global Housing Boom: In Come the Waves, " 16 June 2005. Online: http://www.economist.com/node/4079027 (15 January 2012).

CHART 6

HOMEOWNERSHIP RATES FOR SELECTED YEARS (1940 – 2010)

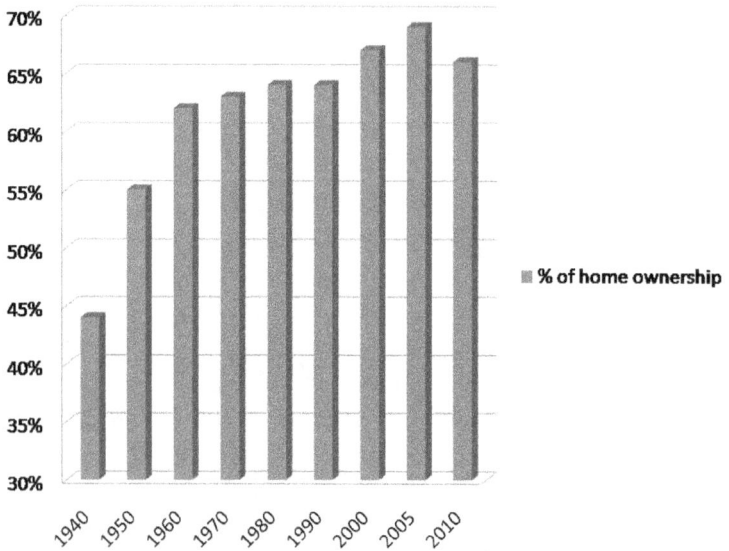

Source: Data adapted from National Association of Realtors. Online:
http://www.realtor.org/sites/default/files/social-benefits-of-stable-housing-2012-04.pdf (12 August 2010).

Note: At the beginning of the 20th century, less than half of all Americans were homeowners.

Approximately 23% of the homes purchased during the housing boom were bought as investment properties. Another 13% was purchased as second homes. Many investors believed that the escalating real estate market was headed for the stars with no recourse and purchased homes that later rented at a loss. Flippers hoping to capitalize purchased homes and resold them prior to completion of construction. Many properties changed hands three or even four times prior to actual occupancy. Lenders and financial institutions were allowed to loosen their guidelines. As a result, an array of new mortgage products entered the real estate market. The new products were riskier than the old ones. Included in the new products was one that allowed borrowers to qualify for jumbo (very large) loans. About 42% of all first-time borrowers and 25% of overall buyers purchased properties with zero down (no down-payment). Aside from the actual cost of the property, the overall mortgage transactions carried a settlement cost made up of fees and expenses in excess of the price of the property. The loose lending procedures allowed investors who did not have enough money to cover their settlement/closing costs to take loans of up to 105% of the value of the property. Any overage in excess of the selling price of the real estate was applied to the closing costs. Many of the borrowers did not understand the characteristics of the fancy, innovative lending products and the meaning of the sophisticated terms such as negative-amortization, interest-only, and adjustable-rate mortgages. However, despite their lack of comprehension in this area, being able to qualify for the loan was a major incentive for the soon-to-be homeowners. Their ignorance to the loan characteristics, mortgage terms, and composition of the figures obscured the fact that the loan products were unsuitable for many of them. They did not have the slightest inkling that their naïve actions could become a catalyst for a major real estate crisis.

Adamu identified many factors as the causes of the real estate crisis. Among the causes highlighted are the following:

1) Poor judgment of both the borrowers and the lenders,

2) Inability of borrowers to meet their loan obligations in a timely manner, and

3) Risky mortgage products that were not understood by the borrowers.

As the government eased the once stringent credit requirements on loans, many lenders were able to extended credit to subprime borrowers who did not have good credit and would otherwise not qualify prior to the amended lending criteria. The new guidelines called for lower interest rates. The drop in rates attracted the subprime borrowers and a flood of first-time homebuyers and other investors swarmed the real estate market.[92]

Real estate prices are driven by supply and demand. If supply is greater than demand, prices will fall; on the contrary, if demand is greater than supply, prices will rise. The market imbalance caused an increase in the price of homes. During the mid-2000s, real estate demand outweighed supply and prices rose sharply. The continuous increase in price created a housing bubble.

Following are some factors that contributed to the demand for houses:

- An increase in population
- An upturn in the economy that created more disposable income for consumers
- Low interest rates
- Low affordable initial monthly payments
- Easy credit
- The relationship between the broker and borrower whereby the borrower was influenced to take on risk
- A lack of financial literacy

Any combination of these forces helped the bubble to rise more rapidly. Before long, the plethora of real estate transactions that resulted from the buying frenzy functioned as helium and quickly inflated the bubble. Forecasters predicted that the prices of homes would become extremely inflated and in order to bring the prices of homes back in line with their values, an intervention in the form of a remarkable event was going to occur. The real estate bubble was getting bigger and bigger. The bigger it got, the more likely it was to explode. When bubbles are created, their natural tendency is to burse sooner or later. The U.S housing bubble burst and the American nation experienced what is

---

[92] Adamu. There were a number of theories that expressed different causes of the mortgage meltdown that in turn triggered a national financial crisis that did not take long to escalate to a global crisis. The boom and bust of the real estate market, particularly subprime lending and high-risk loans, was believed to have been a leading player.

referred to as the largest historical real estate bubble burst. When the bubble exploded, it triggered financial losses to homeowners, mortgage lenders, and investors. Losses began to spiral out of control and created a reversal of many of the variables that caused the burst. For example, the upturn in the economy became a downturn and many individuals lost their jobs. As interest rates rose, the low affordable initial monthly payments adjusted upwards and resulted in larger monthly payments. New lending guidelines were established, the lax credit terms and conditions became more stringent, and the need for education in financial literacy became a heightened concern for everyone.

A number of theories have been identified as factors that caused the mortgage crisis. It is believed that many of the causative factors stemmed from subprime lending and therefore, Bianco (2008) has labeled subprime lending as a major cause of the mortgage meltdown. The steep rise in foreclosures that began in 2006 spiraled out of control in 2007. By the end of that same year, a recession swept across the country and brought with it mass layoffs and unemployment combined with an excessively high rate of home foreclosures. Everyone expected the economy to continue to deteriorate. Billions of dollars were lost in real estate value. This triggered a national mortgage mess that expeditiously globalized by 2008. Overall, it was expected that the foreclosure crisis would result in half-a-million fewer jobs created in 2008. Experts forecasted that billions of dollars in tax revenues would be lost. The prices of homes continued to fall throughout 2008 and job-loss affected many individuals and families. Credit-worthy prime borrowers, now unemployed, began falling behind on their payments. Also, a large number of prime loans made earlier had low initial interest rates that reset to higher interest rates and in turn increased the amount of the monthly payments. The effects of the widespread catastrophe were felt far and wide. The prime borrowers were experiencing the same type of financial stress as the subprime borrowers. The mortgage confusion caused disagreements among borrowers, lenders, financial institutions, and legislators, and produced heated debates over its actual causes and remedies. One very important question remains unanswered: What actually needs to be done in order to fix the mess and move forward?[93]

A gray area in the lending process that is believed to have been a causative factor of the real estate market crash of the mid to late 2000s pertains to the lending disclosures that are required by Congress to be given to the borrowers. The Truth-in-Lending (TIL) is one such disclosure. The TIL consists of important aspects of the loan such as: the amount that was financed, the amount of the required minimum monthly payment, the total number of monthly payments, and the annual percentage rate. Congress designed the TIL to be consumer-friendly and expected that borrowers would easily understand the figures on the TIL.[94]

When a borrower applies for a mortgage, a loan application is completed and the type of loan that best fits the borrower's needs is chosen. Within three days of receipt of the loan application, the lender is required to provide the borrower with several disclosures contain important information and figures about the mortgage. Included in the disclosures is the TIL. The primary reason the government made the TIL mandatory is threefold: 1) to assist the borrower in understanding the costs associated with the loan, 2) reduce confusion, and 3) ensure that the borrower is able to make an informed decision concerning the loan agreement that is being entered into.

Representatives from the governmental agencies that created the TIL were never present during the mortgage transactions and were therefore not able to examine the contents of the TIL after it was populated, or the manner in which the TIL was presented to the borrower. Lenders and

---

[93] Katalina Bianco, "The Subprime Lending Crisis: Causes and Effects of the Mortgage Meltdown," CCH, 2008: 2, 10, 15-16. Online:
http://www.business.cch.com/bankingfinance/focus/news/Subprime_WP_rev.pdf (28 May 2011). At the end of November 2007, it was reported that the subprime mortgage meltdown and resulting foreclosure fallout would have massive economic consequences for the Nation's 361 metro areas.

[94] Jeff Sovern, "Preventing Future Economic Crises Through Consumer Protection Law or How the Truth-in-Lending Act Failed the Subprime Borrowers," 2008. Online:
http://moritzlaw.osu.edu/lawjournal/issues/volume71/number4/sovern.pdf (2 July 2011). Although the borrowers did not comprehend what was stated on the disclosures, they failed to decline the loans and instead, signed for and closed on the unsuitable loans. "It appeared that many borrowers entered into their mortgages without comprehending the terms and the ramifications of those loans."

Title Agents who may have had an interest in the obscurity of the disclosure were the ones responsible for both the preparation and presentation of the disclosure documents to the borrowers. A real estate transaction is the largest financial transaction that most individuals will ever effect. Therefore, the borrowers needed to understand all the details on the disclosures. Most of the borrowers were limited in financial literacy. Knowing quite well that they did not possess the skills necessary to understand the figures on the TIL, many might have lacked interest, avoided reviewing the figures, and overlooked the disclosures. It was the lenders' responsibility to make sure the borrowers understood the contents of the disclosures.[95]

According to Lacko and Pappalardo (2007), the TIL disclosure did not contain all of the information necessary to determine if the borrowers would be able to meet their mortgage obligations.[96] As a result of the inadequacies, many borrowers were unaware that they were being placed in unaffordable loans. Before long, many of the borrowers defaulted on their loan obligations. If many of the borrowers were financially literate and understood the make-up of the figures on the loan disclosures, they would not have signed and agreed to many of the loans, knowing quite well that according to the terms of the loans, they would not be able to meet their obligations in a timely manner. Many sub-prime borrowers were fitted into unsuitable Adjustable Rate Mortgage (ARM) loans. If they did not accept the ARM loans, there would have been a lower rate of default and the financial crisis might have been less severe.

In an effort to examine how well consumers understood the costs on the original TIL disclosures, Lacko and Pappalardo (2007) created a

---

[95] Ibid. Although the borrowers did not comprehend what was stated on the disclosures, they failed to decline the loans and instead, signed for and closed on the unsuitable loans. "It appeared that many borrowers entered into their mortgages without comprehending the terms and the ramifications of those loans.

[96] James M. Lacko and Janis K. Pappalardo, "Improving Consumer Mortgage Disclosures: An Empirical of Current and Prototype Disclosure Forms," Federal Trade Commission bureau of Economic Staff Report, 1. Online: http://www.ftc.gov/os/2007/06/P025505MortgageDisclosureexecutivesummary.pdf (5 August 2011). The United States of America has a long history of mortgage cost disclosure requirements and many legislative and regulatory proposals; however, it has been concluded that the current mortgage cost disclosures fail to convey the key mortgage costs to consumers, and borrowers fail to understand key terms.

prototype TIL and performed a study that compared the original TIL created by the government with the prototype TIL designed by the researchers. In-depth consumer interviews previously conducted during the real estate boom (2004-2005) and quantitative consumer testing were used. A telephone call preceded the interviews, in order to recruit participants who had recently obtained mortgages. Thirty-six borrowers who obtained mortgages within the previous 4 months were selected to participate. Survey instruments were constructed to examine how consumers shopped for mortgages and how well they understood the terms of the loans they were given. The prototype disclosures were developed to compare with the types of loans used in the testing, including: fixed-rate, adjustable-rate, interest-only, balloon payment, bi-weekly payment option, and combination (piggy-back) loans. Half of the participants borrowed from a prime lender. The other half borrowed from a subprime lender. After a series of questions pertaining to the terms of the mortgage loans recently obtained, borrowers who agreed to participate were asked to attend a face-to-face interview and were asked to bring their TIL and other mortgage loan disclosures with them.

A test consisting of 25 questions that pertained to two different loan types was administered to the participants. The first 21 questions addressed simple loans. The last 4 questions addressed loans that had more complex features such as interest only payments with no escrow for taxes and insurance, balloon payments, and prepayment penalties, among other types. The participants were given cost disclosures for two hypothetical mortgage loans and asked a series of questions pertaining to terms such as the loan amounts, settlement costs, charges for optional products and services, up-front costs, interest rates, APRs, cash due at closing, monthly payments, property taxes, homeowners' insurance, balloon payments, and prepayments. The participants were asked to identify which loan had a higher rate and which loan had a lower rate regarding specific costs that were pointed out. Participants were also asked to examine the loans to identify the presence or inclusion of particular costs.

During the testing, half of the participants were given the original TIL disclosure. The other half was given the prototype TIL. The prototype form was simple and straightforward and contained the key costs that needed to be understood by borrowers. Unimportant information was not included on the prototype form. The form was structured in a manner that allowed the various costs to be easily identified. The prototype form also provided many totals, such as the total loan amount rather than the amount financed, and total up-front charges. These figures were not provided on the original TIL disclosure.

The report of the study suggests that borrowers did not understand the costs and terms of the loans as disclosed on the original TIL created by the government and as a result, were not aware that many had been given unsuitable loans. It was crucial that borrowers understood how the loans worked, what types of interest rates they were being offered, what percentage of their income repayment of the mortgage would demand, and exactly what were the details of the various payment options. The findings of the study further suggest that the regular mortgage disclosure forms given to consumers did not include nor fully explained the true costs of the mortgage. The original TIL disclosure failed to simplify the loan process and did not give the borrowers the clarity they needed. Overall, many borrowers were confused by the contents of the original TIL. Following is a listing of other findings:

1) Nearly a quarter (of the participants) could not identify the amount of settlement charges.

2) About a third could not identify the interest rates or which two loans were less expensive, and a third did not recognize that the loans included a large balloon payment or that the loan amounts included money borrowed to pay the settlement charges.

3) Half could not correctly identify the loan amounts.

4) Two-thirds did not recognize that they would be charged a payment penalty if in two years they refinanced with another lender (and a third did not even recognize that they "may" be charged a penalty).

5) Three-quarters did not recognize that substantial charges for optional credit insurance were included in the loans.

6) Almost four-fifths did not know why the interest rate and APR of a loan sometimes differed.

7) Nearly nine-tenths could not identify the total amount of up-front charges in the loan.[97]

Many homeowners lost their homes due to the unsuitability of the loans while many lenders were forced to close their doors.

Another factor that aided and abetted the real estate market failure was laxness in the lending criteria. In the past, borrowers who did not have good credit ratings were rejected for loans altogether. Then, things changed. Lawmakers eased the stringent lending guidelines. Prior to the economic downturn, everyone could qualify for a loan regardless of his or her credit rating. Sub-prime borrowers were regarded as individuals with less-than-desirable credit ratings. Subprime borrowers were given higher interest rates than prime borrowers because of their creditworthiness. There were different classes of subprime borrowers. The borrower who just barely missed getting the prime loan got a lower rate than the borrower who was just out of bankruptcy court. Although everyone qualified for a loan of some type, the interest rates were contingent upon the amount of risk that the lender believed was associated with the loan.

The lenders were negligent regarding the approval of the mortgage loans and failed to ensure that the borrowers would be able to make the payments. The borrowers did not understand the cost of the loans no more than they understood the wide variety of different types of mortgages. They did not possess the financial literacy needed to comprehend the contents of the loan disclosures. If the borrowers understood the figures on the loan documents, they would very well have realized that given their present conditions, they would not be able to fit the monthly payments into their budgets.

Oftentimes, the loans were approved based on very little or no documentation. Some loans were approved based on the borrowers' credit scores. This type of loan was called a "stated income" or a "no-doc" loan. Lenders were allowed to extend credit to borrowers without first

---

[97] Ibid., 7.

verifying their income and other pertinent information. This lending criterion allowed many borrowers to commit to loans for which they would not otherwise qualify. According to the provisions of the Act, lenders are required to make reasonable efforts, in good faith, to investigate whether the borrowers are able to repay the loans. In order to perform this review, a suitability analysis based on verified and documented information regarding the borrower's financial situation is performed. A suitability analysis tells if the loan is suitable for the borrow, and also tells if the borrower will be able to make the payments after the rates reset and the payment amount adjusts upwards, in the case of an ARM loan. During the real estate boom, verification of the borrower's income used to perform the suitability analysis was not required.

By having the privilege to submit undocumented income and not being required to prove the source of their income, the borrowers were encouraged to exaggerate their financial statuses.[98] One major drawback with this type of loan was that the mortgage brokers and other associates of the lenders knew what figures were needed on the mortgage loan applications in order to get the lender's approval. The crooked real estate agents manipulated the figures on the loan documents by performing calculations beforehand to arrive at the required figures then plugged the figures into the TIL to fit the lenders' requirements. The mortgage transactions were unscrupulously done for personal gain.

The financial crisis has been a turning point for most everyone. The crisis brought about many changes within households, societies and governmental agencies. Many borrowers who were unable to meet their financial obligations because of job loss, sickness or inability to work, divorce, failed businesses, or simply because of taking on mortgage loans that were unsuitable, have lost their homes to foreclosure, while lenders apply intense pressure tactics on other borrowers. The borrowers believe

---

[98] The Federal Reserve Bank of San Francisco: "The Subprime Mortgage Market," Annual Report, 2007, 6. Online: http://www.frbsf.org/publications/federalreserve/annual/2007/subprime.pdf (26 August 2011). Borrowers in the alt-A category ordinarily had a higher credit score than borrowers in the subprime category. However, the loans were viewed as nonprime loans because their terms and conditions had specific features such as: very little or no income documentation, high loan-to-value ratio, high payment to income ratio, or purchase of a second home, among other features.

that they are neither directly nor indirectly responsible for the problems caused by the financial dilemma. They believe the source of the problem stems from forces beyond their control. As borrowers read and hear about the collapse of trusted financial institutions, many feel that they were lied to and betrayed by their lenders. The damage caused to borrowers is uncertain. One thing is certain. The financial pains and stressors will continue to be felt indefinitely for years to come and will result in slower economic re-growth. The crisis reminds lawmakers of the importance and need for strong economic policies that protect the public against financial laxness and fraud.[99]

The aftermath of the 2008 economic storm has created feelings of unrest for everyone. As the swells of the financial storm continue to rise, homes and businesses that did not have emergency cash saved up capsize everywhere. Financial structures that did not have solid foundations continue to crumble. The cost of reconstruction is immense. Although the storm-resistant structures that had emergency savings survived, many need repairs. Many individuals who were already experiencing serious financial difficulties prior to the economic storm compounded their problems by taking on additional loans. They borrowed cash with outrageous terms from greedy lenders at inflated interest rates. Before long, the vast majority of the loans turned out to be faulty subprime loans. Such type of lending was not new to the real estate market, its frequency simply multiplied and became common practice. Many of the once trusted lending institutions became rip-off loan sharks who blatantly used sophisticated financial instruments to lure borrowers to agree to unsuitable loan terms. The buyers committed themselves to the loan agreements without understanding the outrageous terms that were set forth on the incomprehensible loan documents. The risky loans were packaged and sold in bulks as investment units or bonds. Being greedy for more and more profits, many of the lenders and other investors purchased the risky loans. Things appeared "too good to be true!"

---

[99] Robert J. Shiller, "The Subprime Solution: How Today's Global Financial Crisis Happened, and What to do About It," (Princeton, NJ, Princeton University Press, 2008, 10). "Homeownership was a worthy and admirable national goal. It demonstrated participation and belonging, and was beneficial to a healthy society."

According to the philosophical concept of "cause and effect," for every action there is an equal and opposite reaction." Before long, a number of the borrowers who did not qualify for the unsuitable loans in the first place defaulted on their loan agreements. They simply could not fit their monthly mortgage obligations into their budgets. The unaffordable payment amounts were budget-busters. Foreclosures began to rise rapidly and caused the value of homes to plummet. As prices continued to drop lower and lower, there was panic everywhere: with homeowners and lending institutions, on Wall Street, and in Washington. The fears turned into an all-out hysteria. Homeowners decided it was not a good thing to continue spending and restrained their spending. The result was a sluggish economy that caused a strain on businesses. Many were compelled to close their doors while others vanished overnight, resulting in massive layoffs everywhere. As unemployment rose higher and higher, the foreclosure cycle continued to spin out of control and real estate value continued to plummet.

Homeownership, considered to be an individual "right" in the United States, was over-promoted in the mid-2000s. The assumed privilege led many to believe that everyone should be a homeowner. In those days, everyone everywhere could qualify for one type of mortgage loan or another. This set the stage for an influx of homeownership. The overly large demand for homes outweighed the supply of homes and caused home prices to soar to an all-time high. Despite the escalating prices, the homeownership rate continued to rise. "Overly aggressive mortgage lenders, compliant appraisers, and complacent borrowers" fueled the housing boom. The mortgage originators who did not plan to keep the loans but quickly pass them on to investors had no concerns for repayment risks and consistently bypassed verifying the borrowers' income with the Internal Revenue Service, even in cases where the borrowers had given authorization to do so. The loans were afterwards packaged, sold to financial institutions, and then resold on Wall Street, to sophisticated investors around the globe. In doing so, the stage was set for a global financial crisis.[100]

---

[100] Shiller, 12 & 13.

With the rapid rise in real estate prices, borrowers who purchased homes during 2006 and 2007 when the prices were extremely inflated simply paid too much. When prices fell soon thereafter, many borrowers owed more than their homes were worth and needed help with bringing their outstanding loan balances in line with the value of their homes. Shiller (2008) recommends that the government encourage lenders to educate borrowers regarding their specific situations and reward lenders for their time and monies spent to educate the borrowers. Education in and of itself will not solve the problem. Cash in the form of bailout assistance is needed to rectify the situations. The expectation is that the cash assistance will fix the short-term problem. However, in an attempt to prevent a reoccurrence of this problem, a long-term solution is needed. After educating the financially illiterate borrowers, continuing education programs should be offered nationwide. Shiller (2008) believes that sound financial principles should be taught to societies everywhere with the use of every type of modern technology that exists. Education in financial literacy will not stop the next bubble from rising but will allow consumers to efficiently and effectively respond to the bubble or any similar incidences in the future. Thereby, "after-the-fact scurrying for quick fixes" will be avoided.[101]

With day-to-day financial decisions being more and more complex, the deficiency is leading to a rising trend of sublevel behaviors such as compulsive spending. Such behaviors result in high levels of debt. In an attempt to bridge the gap between financial literacy and illiteracy, policy makers have mandated that education in financial literacy become part of the curricula of many primary and secondary schools. However, there is concern that many full-time students who are not employed and are not earning income while studying will not have money to use as a practice tool. As a result, students in this group will not retain the lessons for future application to their finances when they became employed. Furthermore, there is the possibility that the education and skills acquired today might not lend to the making of solid financial decisions in the future, due to the never-ending array of new and improved financial products that continue to enter the financial markets. For example,

---

[101] Ibid., 89-90.

individuals are now faced with a new and much wider array of responsibilities and opportunities including retirement planning. In order to successfully plan for retirement, financial sophistication is a primary requirement. The level of financial literacy education that many possess is not enough to warrant financial sophistication. Therefore, many individuals who are required to manage their retirement plans are not trained to do so.

Behavioral Finance

ACCORDING TO FEFFER AND STANTON, financial literacy in and of itself is not enough. Individuals who know what needs to be done yet fail to take action have a "knowing-doing problem." Knowing and doing are two totally different concepts. There is a wide variance between knowing what to do in theory and acting upon the knowledge obtained by applying the practicalities to everyday life. The deviation between knowing and doing is far greater than the difference between ignorance and knowledge.[102] Many individuals fall prey to common traits such as procrastination and distraction. Some become overwhelmed with the details of decision-making. Yet, others yield to persuasions such as spending instead of saving. Although "people may know which course is best for them, (they fail to) follow through."[103]

Individuals need to be aware of their capabilities. In order to be able to turn knowledge into action individuals must have the following three qualities:

1) they must be aware of the limits of their capabilities,
2) they must have access to structures that will assist them with the transition from knowledge to action, and
3) they must have the discipline to raise the bar against social norms.[104]

---

[102] Jeffrey Feffer & Robert I. Sutton, "The Knowing Doing Gap, " Harvard Business School Press, 2000, 1. Online: http://toolkitforplcs.pbworks.com/w/file/fetch/40397385/The%20Knowing%20Doing%20Gap.pdf (20 March 2012).

[103] Barbara Kiviat & Jonathan Morduch, "From Financial Literacy to Financial Action," McGraw-Hill Research Foundation, 9 January 2012, 3. Online: http://mcgraw-hillresearchfoundation.org/wp-content/uploads/2012/01/Financial_Literacy_WP.pdf (20 March 2012).

[104] Ibid.

For example, if an under-banked individual wants to save $1000.00 to purchase a computer in 5 months, that person must know that he or she is able to set aside $200.00 each month while continuing to meet other cost-of-living obligations in a timely manner. That individual should also have access to some type of structured program or service such as a payroll direct deposit program that will encourage that person to save the amount required to accomplish the goal. Lastly, the individual must be disciplined and avoid letting good intentions get sidetracked by common pitfalls. For example, he or she must be careful not to follow the crowd, succumb to herd mentality, and manage his or her finances like everyone else who shops first and saves later.

Junior Achievement describes financial literacy as two-dimensional, consisting of both a theoretical or educational side, and a practical or action side. The skills learned on the theoretical side are applied on the action side, processed, and then outputted in the form of wise, informed, sound, financial decisions that include how to budget, spend, save, and invest. The theoretical and practical sides of financial literacy possess an extremely close hand-in-glove relationship. In order for individuals to be successful at personal finance, both of the dimensions or sides (theoretical and practical) of financial literacy must collaborate and work in harmony with one another, as action helps to crystallize or define theory. When theory and practice are uncoupled they lose support for one another and practice can then be defined as being subjective.[105]

After being taught the theories of personal finance, an individual must develop a heart-felt desire to change. Changing lifestyles or habits can be very difficult. A study was performed by Xiao, O'Neill, Procaska, Kerbel, Brenan, and Bristow (2000), to investigate "why some people make

---

[105] Financial Literacy, "Foundation for Success: A global Perspective," Junior Achievement, 2. Online: http://www.ja.org/ (31 March 2012). Many youth have a woefully inadequate grasp of the essential knowledge required to make the most basic, yet critical financial decisions. Financial literacy would allow them to both survive and thrive in their corner of the world, and make informed decisions about budgeting, credit, spending, saving and preparing to prosper in their retirement years. Financial literacy had long been held as one of the most critical competencies required for young people. Education in financial literacy would equip the youths with the skills needed to survive in an ever complex and changing global economy.

successful behavior changes while others, who say they want to change, never seem to get around to it." The Transtheoretical Model of Change (TTM) developed by Prochaska and his colleagues was used in the study. The aim of the study was two-fold: 1) to discuss how to apply the TTM to the financial behaviors of individuals and 2) to find out what change processes are the most effective when used by individuals who were serious about changing their habits. Behavior change was defined as a process, not an event. According to the TTM, the five stages of change individuals encounter while moving through the change process on their way to change are:

1) Pre-contemplation – The individual may or may not be aware that a problem exist
2) Contemplation – The individual is aware of the problem and the need to change
3) Determination – The individual has made a decision to change
4) Action – The individual has devised a plan to make the necessary changes
5) Maintenance – Change has been achieved; positive behaviors are in place[106]

Overall, the report of the study recommends the revision of many of the existing financial education programs to include the TTM to be applied to the behaviors of individuals. Individuals are unique and therefore, they are at different stages of change. In order to understand the extent of an individual's determination to change and also to measure the stage of change, it is necessary to adopt the processes of the TTM to the financial education program.

Quite similar to the combining of theory and practice in financial literacy, economics and psychology have merged and have reproduced a new discipline called Behavioral Finance (BF). Financial literacy and BF complement one another. However, they are not synonymous terms.

---

[106] Jing J. Xiao, Barbara O'Neill, Janice M. Prochaska, Claudia Kerbel, Patricia Brennan, and Barbara Bristow, "Application of the Tanstheoretical Model of Change to Financial Behaviors," Consumer Interests Annual, 2001, Vol. 47, 2. Online: http://165.230.176.46/money2000/pdfs/acci01m2k-proceedings.pdf (30 May 2012).

Both disciplines are separate and distinct from one another. Lessons on these topics should be blended and presented as a unified lesson on financial education.

Behavioral finance is a science that explains the specific behaviors of individuals. This field of study combines the behavioral traits of individuals with the study of economics and finance, and uses the results to explain why people behave the way they do and choose the economic decisions they make. The new discipline is described as being scientific as well as practical. The field of study deals with the actual behaviors of individuals. BF investigates the social, cognitive and emotional factors that affect the economic decisions of individuals, and the consequences of these decisions.

Individuals make decisions intuitively or rationally. After realizing that a wrong decision was made, most individuals try to justify their actions, even if the results turn out to be costly. Such deceptive patterns of behaviors have the tendency to repeat themselves. Self-deception can go on indefinitely and because many individuals do not want to face the truth, they choose to continue in this vein.[107] Decision-making is based on three factors: perception, processing, and evaluation. These criteria influence one another. Therefore, it is difficult or almost impossible to examine each one separately.

People will not voluntarily change their behaviors unless one of the following two things occurs:

1) they are awarded incentives that are well worth the change in behavior, or
2) making the change is extremely easy, it becomes compelling and irresistible.

Change can be difficult even when the process is easy. When change occurs, it is normal for individuals to experience feelings of detachment and lonesomeness. Therefore, instead of going through the motions of change, many defer to follow the crowd. They are inclined to associate with others and behave like one another without having any type of

---

[107] Goldberg, Joachim & Von Nitzsch, Rudiger, *Behavioral Finance,* (John Wiley and Sons, Inc., New York, 2001), 87.

planned direction – they simply follow or mimic one another's actions. This specific type of behavior called "herd behavior" or "herd mentality" was clearly seen in the mid-2000s during the real estate boom and bust. Individuals behave like herds of animals for the following two reasons:

1) **Social Pressure** – In order to join the group, an individual is pressured into behaving like the rest of the group. They must conform to the group norms.

2) **Anchoring** – Individuals find a point of reference in their minds, for example, they decide how much something is worth, and they stick with it. It then becomes impossible to get them to change their minds.[108]

Social pressure is also experienced by many adolescent individuals, in the form of a powerful influential force called: peer pressure. Parents must dominate this force with consistent lessons in money management. Regardless of the level of financial literacy, social pressure affects everyone and is a strong influence for displays of herd mentality.

Although consequential decision-making habits such as procrastination, distraction, or even spending instead of saving sometimes spiral out of control, these habits are within individuals' control and can be harnessed.[109] Initiatives to control such habits, encourage discipline, and assist individuals with doing what needs to be done should be implemented. For example, individuals who are not disciplined to save for retirement should have access to a direct deposit system that captures a

---

[108] Michelle Osak, "Behavioral Economics 101: Influencing Consumer Choice," Financial Post, 8 July 2010. Online: http://business.financialpost.com/2010/07/08/behavioral-economics-101-influencing-customer-choice/ (18 March 2012).

[109] "McGraw-Hill Research Foundation White Paper Calls for New Approach to Creating Effective Financial Literacy Program," McGraw Hill Research Foundation, 9 January 2012. Online: http://mcgraw-hillresearchfoundation.org/2012/01/09/mcgraw-hill-research-foundation-white-paper-calls-for-new-approach-to-creating-effective-financial-literacy-programs/ (16 June 2012). "People may know which course is best for them…but still don't manage to follow through. Human beings are social creatures, and social norms often act against financial prudence. But norms can also be harnessed to promote better financial decision-making."

pre-tax portion of their income and deposits it in a restricted retirement account.

Although the financially illiterate borrowers might not have access to systems that encouraged discipline, many can be faulted for their contributions to the financial crisis. The borrowers fell into one of two categories. There were those in the first category who were naïve to the entire transaction and were simply interested in two things: 1) being told the good news that their loans were approved and 2) being shown where to sign their names on the documents. Many of the borrowers might have thought that the manipulation of the numbers was normal. Despite the fact that they did not understand how the figures were derived, many were aware from the discussions that their income was a lie and was stated much higher than their actual earnings.

The borrowers shared mixed emotions. On the one hand they were concerned about rising property values and on the other hand they were excited about wanting to realize the American Dream. Thus, many looked the other way and fraudulently signed the liar-loan documents. Commonsense should have warned the unsophisticated buyers that many of them might not be able to meet their repayment obligations. When millions of borrowers found it impossible to make their mortgage loan payments, they defaulted. The succession of delinquencies caused the real estate market to plummet and many mortgage brokers and lenders went out of business. As the display of gross national financial ignorance continues, it appears that James Truslow Adams' ideals of the American dream ". . . of a land in which life should be better and richer and fuller for everyone, with opportunities for each according to ability or achievement," ended prior to the real estate crisis.[110]

---

[110] Jonas Clarke, "In Search of the American Dream." The Atlantic Magazine, June 2007. Online: http://www.theatlantic.com/magazine/archive/2007/05/in-search-of-the-american-dream/5921/ (31 March 2012).

Chapter Three

THIS CHAPTER CONSISTS of a detailed description of the design and methodology used to accomplish the results of this research. The focus of the study was to investigate the need for education in financial literacy as a lifelong endeavor. The study focused on any possible relationships that exist between the slumped economy and financial literacy, and researched any correlation that exists between financial literacy and behavioral finance.

STUDY DESIGN AND METHODOLOGY

In order to maintain the focus of the study and determine the need for continuing education in financial literacy, the study used a quantitative research design and methodology that consisted of both primary and secondary data. The quantitative design was chosen because it was the most appropriate method to use in order to determine the relationships or associations between the variables in the study. The quantitative study design correlated the results of the survey instruments and thereby maintained the focus of the study. The primary information was gathered from questionnaires constructed in the form of Likert scale survey instruments, administered to a sample of ninety-eight subjects eighteen years and older, who participated in three financial seminars held during 2010. The secondary information was selected from the output of researchers, including case studies, reviews, and reports on people's behaviors. The overall results of this study are derived from the participants' responses to the surveys, and the analyses and interpretations of the reports / findings of other researchers. The results have been analyzed and determined to be valuable tools for use by educators, in their consideration for a curriculum in financial education.

POPULATION

The target subset in this study was comprised of ninety-eight subjects made up of pastors, engineers, architects, musicians, teachers, students, and community members. All of the participants were eighteen years and older and were selected on the basis of their participation in three financial seminars held during 2010. The statistics gathered from the surveys are displayed in the Tables listed in the Table of Contents.

SAMPLE

A convenience sample was used to represent the nation's population. It was not ideal for the researcher to test the entire nation, therefore, the subjects in the sample were selected because they were readily available and the easiest to recruit for the study.

DATA COLLECTION

The data used in this study included both primary and secondary sources. The primary data consisted of the direct, personal responses obtained by the researcher from the participants who attended the financial seminars. The primary data was collected on questionnaires constructed in the form of Likert scale survey instruments, designed by the researcher. The surveys were administered to the subset described above (ninety-eight subjects, eighteen years and older, who participated in three financial seminars held during 2010). The survey instruments were made up of information gleaned by the researcher during discussions with attendees from financial seminars held earlier. A financial education curriculum was also used as a source for some of the content areas found on the questionnaires. The aim of the questionnaires was to determine the perceptions, attitudes, and knowledge of the participants, regarding personal finance. The first survey instrument consisted of 10 closed-ended questions that tested the participants' knowledge of basic financial principles. Each question required a "yes" or "no" answer.[111] The second and third instruments, also in the form of questionnaires that contained 10 questions each, were designed to capture the personal theologies behind

---

[111] Each of the 10 questions was awarded one point. The questions were structured to test the participants' knowledge of basic financial principles. To be considered financially fit, a participant had to answer at least 9 of the 10 questions correctly.

the various styles of personal financial management, and the participants' opinions regarding their need for continuing education in financial literacy.

The secondary data was gathered from the output of past researchers and included case studies, reviews, articles, unpublished reports, and published books.

OBSERVATION

Face-to-face interviews were held with randomly selected participants prior to the administration of the surveys. Mental notes were taken during the interviews, along with keen observations of the movements and gestures of the interviewees. Some of the qualities noted included behaviors, attitudes, and motivations. Communication was found to be very effective during the interviews. The participants displayed a high level of interest in participation and expressed anticipation of the financial knowledge they expected to acquire during the seminars. Many went on to discuss how they would apply the nuggets gleaned during the seminar to their daily personal financial management styles.

LIMITATIONS

The following three limitations were noted:

1) The surveys were not blind instruments. Prior to completing the surveys, the contents were discussed with the participants who were informed that all information they provided would remain confidential, except their scores would be interpreted in bar graphs.

2) The surveys were designed to provide relevant data on the issue of financial literacy and practical money skills across the nation.

3) The subset consisted of a small number of participants who represented the overall population. In the future, the

researcher would like to distribute surveys to a much larger sample, perhaps electronically through email or telephone surveys, to get a wider range of responses. That would allow for a better representation of the overall population.

4) The subset consisted of individuals who were all interested in attending financial seminars to learn how to become better personal financial managers.

Analysis and Interpretation

ANALYSES OF THE RESPONSES solicited from the attendees of the 3 financial seminars held during 2010 were performed. A total of 22, 34, and 42 participants attended Seminars 1, 2, and 3, respectively. Survey Instrument 1 - Questionnaire #1 was used during Seminar 1, Survey Instrument 2 - Questionnaire #2 was used during Seminar 2, and Survey Instrument 3 - Questionnaire #3 was used during Seminar 3. Analysis of the questionnaires was performed by tabulating each response in an excel spreadsheet. The numbers were added up to ascertain that there were 22, 34, and 42 answers, respectively for each of the 10 questions on each of the 3 survey instruments used during the seminars. A percentage was assigned to each answer.

Survey Instrument 1 – Questionnaire #1 was analyzed first. The "Yes" answers were totaled and the "No" answers were totaled. A percentage was assigned to the "Yes" answers and a percentage was assigned to the "No" answers for a total of 100% for both "Yes" and "No" answers. The total for the "Yes" answers was divided by 22 (the number of participants). The total for the "No" answers was also divided by 22. The resulting percentages were grafted in the Table #12 listed in the Table of Contents.

Survey Instrument 2 – Questionnaire #2 was analyzed next. The answers for each category (Strongly Disagree, Disagree, Undecided, Agree, Strongly Agree) were added up and the result was divided by 34 (the number of participants). This step was repeated 10 times for each question. The resulting percentages were grafted in Table #13 listed in the Table of Contents.

Survey Instrument 3 – Questionnaire #3 was analyzed next. The answers for each category (Always, Usually, Sometimes, Seldom, Never) were added up and the results were divided by 42 (the number of participants). This step was repeated 10 times for each question. The resulting percentages were grafted in Table #14 listed in the Table of Contents.

INTERPRETATIONS: SURVEY INSTRUMENT 1

1. Thirty-six percent of the respondents had savings, checking, and retirement accounts. The other 64% did not have all 3 of those accounts in place. During the face-to-face interviews, the researcher was informed that the majority of participants did not have established retirement accounts.

2. Less than one-fourth (23%) of the respondents admitted that their monthly income was in excess of their monthly expenses. The other 77% of respondents had expenses that outweighed their incomes each month.

3. Eighteen percent of the respondents had an idea of what their current net worth was. The remaining 62% did not know their net worth.

4. Twenty-seven percent paid monthly credit card balances in full; 73% did not.

5. Nine percent had a working spending plan or budget in place whereas the other 91% had no order to the allocation of their finances.

6. Eighteen percent of the respondents reported that they had enough insurance in place to cover their families in case of an emergency; the other 82% did not have enough insurance to cover their families.

7. None of the participants understood how compound interest worked and could not differentiate between simple and compound interest.

8. None of the participants understood the time value of money.

9. None of the participants had a "last will and testimony" or a "living will" and could not explain the difference between the two documents.

10. Nine percent of the participants had their documents in order; the other 91% were like most everyone else, disorganized.

QUESTIONNAIRE 1

Survey Instrument 1 – Questionnaire #1 Financial Fitness Quiz		YES	NO
1	You have these accounts savings, checking, and retirement.	8	14
2	Your monthly income is in excess of your monthly expenses	5	17
3	You know your current net worth	4	18
4	You pay credit card balances in full each month	6	16
5	You have a working spending plan (budget)	2	20
6	You have enough insurance set in place	4	18
7	You understand simple and compound interest	0	22
8	You understand the time value of money	0	22
9	You have a "last will and testament" and a "living will"	0	22
10	Your documents are organized	2	20

TABLE 12

RESULTS FROM SURVEY INSTRUMENT 1

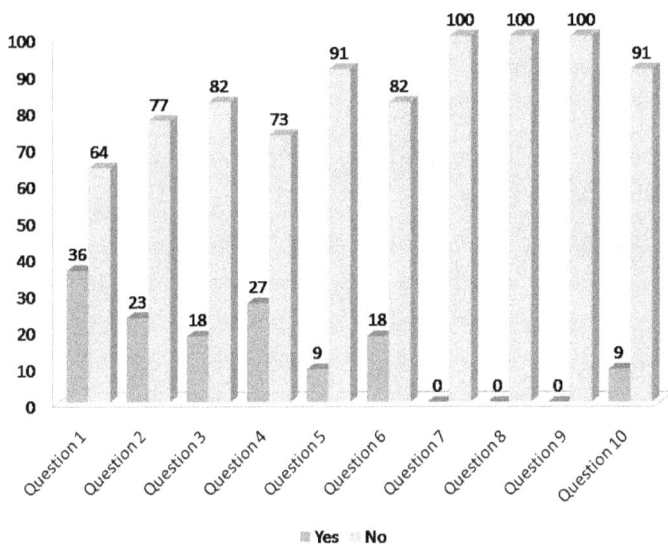

INTERPRETATIONS: SURVEY INSTRUMENT 2

The responses to the questions on Questionnaire #2 are analyzed below:

1. All of the respondents strongly agreed that through financial literacy education, everyone would be equipped with the tools necessary to make informed financial decisions.

2. The majority, 88% strongly agreed and the remaining 12% agreed that financial literacy education would help individuals and families to achieve their financial goals.

3. Seventy-nine percent and 21% strongly agreed and agreed, respectively, that financial literacy education should be offered on a continual basis.

4. The participants unanimously strongly agreed that successful personal financial management was of extreme importance.

5. Almost all of the participants, 91%, strongly disagreed and the other 9% disagreed that employees of financial institutions were the only individuals who needed to understand financial concepts such as simple and compound interest.

6. Once more there was unanimous decision that consumers needed to understand basic financial concepts – 100% of the participants strongly agreed.

7. Regarding confidence in the way they managed their finances, 70% of the respondents strongly agreed that they were doing a good job, 15% agreed, and only 6% disagreed expressed a lack of confidence in managing their finances.

8. Most individuals did not have a working budget. Sixty-two percent strongly disagreed sticking to a budget and 23% disagreed. Nine percent agreed only 6% strongly agreed sticking to a budget when managing their finances.

9. Everyone strongly agreed that financial literacy and practical money skills were compliments of one another.

10. Ninety-one percent of the respondents strongly agreed that financial literacy should begin at home as early as possible and the remaining 9% agreed.

QUESTIONNAIRE 2

There are a number of different opinions about whether financial literacy education should be offered as continuing education courses on an ongoing basis. (Financial Literacy means having the knowledge and ability to understand financial theories, make informed financial decisions, and take effective actions regarding the current and future use of money, with an awareness of the possible consequences.)

Please use the following scale to answer the questions:

1	2	3	4	5
Strongly Disagree	Disagree	Undecided	Agree	Strongly Agree

	Question	Strongly Disagree	Disagree	Undecided	Agree	Strongly Agree
1	The primary aim of financial literacy education is to equip individuals and families with the tools needed to make wise financial decisions	0	0	0	0	34
2	Education in financial literacy allows individuals and families to accumulate assets and achieve their financial goals.	0	0	0	4	30
3	Continuing education in Financial Literacy should be offered at least annually.	0	0	0	7	27
4	It is extremely important to be able to properly manage your finances.	0	0	0	0	34
5	Only those who work in financial institutions need to understand financial concepts such as simple and compound interest.	31	3	0	0	0
6	Consumers do not need to understand basic financial concepts	34	0	0	0	0
7	I am confident about the way I manage my finances.	0	2	0	5	27
8	When managing my finances, I stick to my working budget	21	8	0	3	2

	Question	Strongly Disagree	Disagree	Undecided	Agree	Strongly Agree
9	Financial literacy and practical money skills compliment one another.	0	0	0	0	34
10	Financial literacy education should begin as early as possible, preferably at home.	0	0	0	3	31

TABLE 13

RESULTS FROM SURVEY INSTRUMENT 2

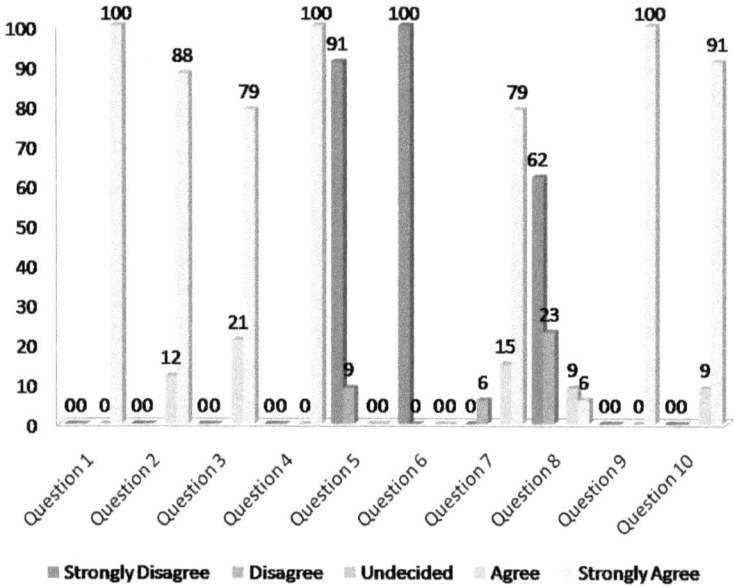

■ Strongly Disagree   ■ Disagree   ■ Undecided   ■ Agree   ■ Strongly Agree

INTERPRETATIONS: SURVEY INSTRUMENT 3

The responses to the questions on Questionnaire #2 are analyzed below:

1. Eighty-eight percent of the respondents believed that financial literacy education always gave individuals the ability to make better financial choices, and 12% believed financial literacy education usually gave individuals such ability.

2. The majority, 86% believed that financial literacy education should always begin at home and 14% believed that it usually should begin at an early age at home.

3. The respondents unanimously agreed that financial literacy always included earning, spending, and saving.

4. Of the respondents, 90% agreed that financial literacy always encouraged paying off credit card debt in full each month and 10% agreed that such education usually encouraged paying credit cards in full each month.

5. A wide variance was found regarding decision-making for the upper, middle, and lower class of individuals. Five percent, 19%, 40%, 24%, and 12%, respectively, believed that the different classes of individuals always, usually, sometimes, seldom, and never, had the same types of financial decisions to make.

6. Everyone believed that effective budgeting allowed individuals to become debt-free and plan for the future.

7. Once again, everyone believed that having a large volume of debt and filing for bankruptcy evidenced the need for education in financial literacy.

8. A wide variance was again seen in the participants' focus regarding their personal finances. Seventeen percent, 33%, 26%, 19%, and 5%, respectively, felt that they always, usually, sometimes, seldom, and never got sidetracked when managing their personal finances.

9. The entire group of participants agreed that they lived in a fast-paced culture that did not support delayed-gratification, and was, therefore, not conducive to personal financial management.

10. The participants were asked to rate their financial management influence on those around them. This question also had varying responses. None, however, believed that their behaviors had absolutely no influence on others. They all believed they influenced others to some degree. Thirty-three percent, 21%, 36%, and 10%, respectively, believed their financial management styles always, usually, sometimes, or seldom influenced others.

QUESTIONNAIRE 3

There are a number of different opinions about whether financial literacy education should be offered as continuing education courses on an ongoing basis. For purposes of this survey, financial literacy means having the knowledge and ability to understand financial theories, make informed financial decisions, and take effective actions regarding the current and future use of money, with an awareness of the possible consequences.

Please use the following scale to answer the questions:

1	2	3	4	5
Always	Usually	Sometimes	Seldom	Never

		Always	Usually	Sometimes	Seldom	Never
1	Personal financial literacy is the ability to understand and manage money, in order to be able to make better financial choices.	37	5	0	0	0
2	Financial literacy teaching should begin at an early age at home, then in school, and should continue on to adulthood.	36	6	0	0	0
3	Financial literacy includes earning, spending, and saving.	42	0	0	0	0
4	Financial Literacy encourages paying off credit card debt in full every month.	38	4	0	0	0
5	People in the upper, middle, and lower class have mostly the same financial decisions to make.	2	8	17	10	5

		Always	Usually	Sometimes	Seldom	Never
6	We should aim to budget effectively, get out of debt, and plan for the future.	42	0	0	0	0
7	High rates of personal debt and bankruptcy are evidence of the need for education in financial literacy.	7	14	11	8	2
8	We tend to get sidetracked easily when it comes to personal financial management.	40	0	0	0	0
9	The habits of our fast-paced culture that demands we get everything we want NOW, is bad for personal finance.	40	0	0	0	0
10	Our financial behaviors have a ripple effect on those around us.	14	9	15	4	0

TABLE 14

RESULTS FROM SURVEY INSTRUMENT 3

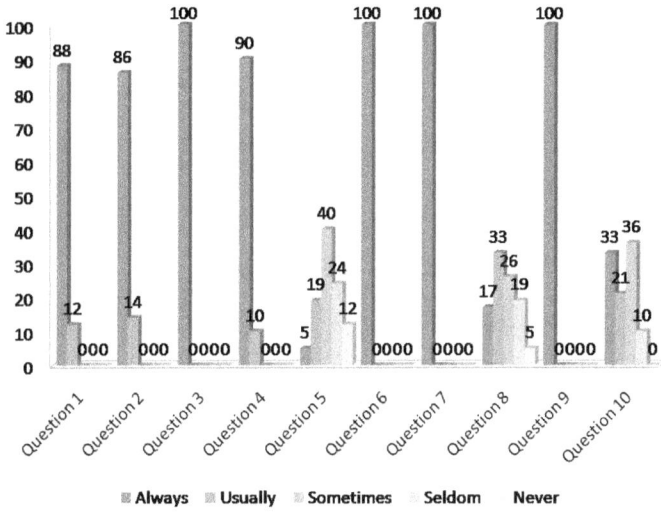

Always   Usually   Sometimes   Seldom   Never

Chapter Four

FINDINGS AND INTERPRETATIONS

THIS CHAPTER CONSISTS of the patterns and trends that were discovered, identified, and interpreted. The findings in this study are used as empirical evidence against which the hypotheses are tested, in order to draw conclusions. Analysis of the primary data (3 surveys administered during the 3 seminars held in 2010) reveals the following:

Questionnaire # 1 - More than 60% of the individuals and families access only limited services (checking and savings accounts) offered by financial institutions and many do not have retirement accounts. Individuals do not understand how to calculate simple or compound interest, neither do they understand the time value of money. A larger number, 91%, do not use a budget or spending plan to bring order to their finances. Such disorganization explains why 77% say they have a negative cash flow each month. Aside from not managing their finances in an orderly manner, most everyone, 91%, did not have a filing system.

Questionnaires # 2 and #3 – The questions on the second and third questionnaires somewhat mirrored one another. The majority of respondents for both surveys agreed that everyone desirous of obtaining training in financial literacy should be given the opportunity to do so. Reinforcement in such training should be done on a continual basis and would, in turn, support better decision-making that would lead to the realization of financial goals.

A review of the secondary data (case studies, reviews, articles, unpublished reports, and published books) identifies low levels of financial literacy nationwide. Acute cases are found to be common-placed among the under-banked and unbanked individuals and families. Therefore, financial literacy is found to be of extreme necessity for the wellbeing of individuals and families and as such, is found to be of heightened concern to governmental officials, educational organizations, school boards, community partners, and families. Although a rapid spread of financial literacy programs are promoted by both public and private organizations, many individuals and families fail to take the initiative to obtain education in personal financial management. From an evaluation of the various efforts, it does not appear that the rate of financial literacy is improved. A closer look at personal financial management shows that individuals and families with limited or no financial literacy training are unable to differentiate between a need and a want and, as such, fail to make prudent decisions. Instead, they make bad financial decisions that usually result in skyrocketing charges. The under-banked and unbanked individuals are found to thrive in neighborhoods that are serviced by high-cost financial predators such as loan-sharks. Financial activities with these unscrupulous predators produced negative results with negative consequences.

After attending financial literacy training seminars, individuals exhibited various types of behaviors. Some failed to grasp the concepts taught and therefore did not comprehend the lessons. Others comprehended the rudimentary concepts but needed reinforcement through continued education. A third group of individuals understood the concepts and skills taught but were not able to transform the financial knowledge obtained into action steps. Individuals in the third group were not self-starters and displayed lackadaisical qualities. Many displayed the need for structures that would assist in turning knowledge into action. Not only did they need to be told what to do, they also needed to be told how to do it. They did not appear to have purpose and needed access to particular services. For example, in order to get the third group of individuals to establish and maintain savings accounts or contribute to individual retirement accounts, access to services such as payroll deduction and direct deposit was necessary. Through the utilization of such services, the action steps necessary for successful personal financial management would be implemented.

A large number of individuals do not manage their finances with the use of a working spending plan. Many do not earn enough to cover their monthly expenses. Due to feelings of discomfort when forced to use basic banking services such as opening and maintaining a savings and/or a checking account, numerous individuals fail to engage the services of formal financial institutions. They do not understand how investments such as money market accounts or certificate of deposits work. They do not understand interest calculations. They are hesitant to engage in transaction accounts (savings and checking) and investments such as certificate of deposits, because they do not understand the concepts involved. They fail to bring order to their finances with the use of a budget either because they never received training in this area or do not feel comfortable when working with budgets because they need reinforcement. They do not possess the solid financial literacy substructure necessary to train their children in these areas. Many parents are not able to teach the theories and practicalities of financial literacy to their off-springs. Due to their lack of financial literacy, they are not able to be good examples for their children.

A strong correlation is traced between limited financial literacy and excessive borrowing. Americans with limited financial literacy find it hard to save. They spend more than they make. Those who are approved for loans, borrow excessively. After racking up a mountain of bills, they are unable to cover themselves against unforeseen and unexpected perils such as foreclosure, job loss, sickness, or the inevitable retirement years. A strong relationship is also found between financial literacy and obligation to high-cost mortgages. Individuals with limited financial literacy are usually members of low-income households who get higher interest rates along with other costs such as insurances, due to the risky nature of their loans. A similar relationship exists between financial literacy and debt literacy. Individuals with limited financial literacy do not understand the interest rate concept. Yet, many borrow money to borrow money. For example, many individuals use credit cards to pay for the down-payment on real estate or automobiles. They end up being obligated to repay the credit card while simultaneously repaying the mortgage or automobile loan. If individuals could not afford the down-payment, how will they ever be able to afford to meet the two resulting payments?

A relationship also exists between financial literacy and behavioral finance. This relationship was prominent among all classes of individuals. Traces of herd mentality and peer pressure regarding homeownership were observed. For example, many of the borrowers succumbed to herd behavior and boarded the train that was headed to the real estate festival where everyone was having fun house-shopping, knowing fully well that they did not have the necessary resources and could not financially afford to purchase a home. Thus, they signaled the need for education in financial literacy. An association exists between financial literacy and behavioral finance wherein individuals behave like members of herds and follow the actions of one another. There is an extremely small difference in the rate of financial literacy between individuals with and without college education. Financial literacy does, however, decrease with age. A pronounced distinction between knowing and doing was observed. Individuals are challenged by turning knowledge of financial literacy into action steps.

Overall, financial literacy is identified as a major determinant for wholesome, sound lifestyles and, therefore, has a direct relationship with the well-being of individuals, families, communities, and the overall national economy. Financial literacy allows individuals to make informed decisions and bring order to their finances by creating and maintaining spending plans, while simultaneously avoiding severe potential backlashes or pitfalls, as a result of mismanaged personal finances.

Chapter Five

CONCLUSIONS AND RECOMMENDATIONS

RECENTLY, AMERICA PLUNGED into a financial crisis that is considered to be the most severe since the great depression of the 1920s and 1930s. In the aftermath of the crisis as the economy continues its downward plight, debt (both public and private) soars at an all-time high. Businesses large and small continue to go under and a record number of homes are lost to foreclosures and short sales. A large number of individuals join the unemployment line. People's greatest fear is that the worst is yet to come! From a review of the nation's history and according to the cyclical laws of nature, it has been concluded that the financial crisis is not the first and will not be the last of its kind. The American nation continues to experience a repetition of things and both the economy and the lifestyles of individuals and families continue to rise and fall. The Bible tells us that there is a time and a season for everything.[112] The ebbs and flows experienced by Americans are simply the different seasons of life. Individuals may not be able to change the seasons in their lives; nonetheless, they can become empowered to make good choices that will positively affect how they survive in times of unfavorable seasons. None of these times and seasons are new.[113] Birds flew before airplanes and whales existed before submarines. However, as things continue to replicate themselves, they get worse. Likewise, as history continues to repeat itself, each new generation continues to disobey biblical instructions and mistrust God.

---

[112] Ecc. 3.1: "To everything there is a season, and a time to every purpose under the heaven."

[113] Ecc. 1.9 & 10: "That which has been is what will be, that which is done is what will be done, and there is nothing new under the sun. Is there anything of which it may be said: see, this is new? It has already been in ancient times before us."

CONCLUSIONS

A lot of literature that supports many causes of the existing financial crisis has recently emerged and debate about the causes continues. The findings of this research report indicate that the following two concepts are proximate causes directly linked to the financial crisis: 1) Americans have turned away from God and have traded their trust in God for trust in material possessions. This has caused the nation to fall from grace, and 2) there is an extremely low rate of financial literacy among Americans. This deficiency functions as fuel for the blazing fires of the financial crisis. The purpose of this study was to investigate the extent of the effects that turning away from God coupled with the lack of financial literacy have on the financial crisis. The following conclusions were drawn from the findings summarized in chapter four.

After careful analysis of the data collected it was concluded that the nation of America is experiencing a financial crisis primarily because many have changed their courses and have turned away from God. They no longer place their trust in Him. They have lost sight of their heritage founded on Biblical principles. They have abandoned God and the American motto: "In God We Trust." Whereas the forefathers sought God and His grace, Americans now seek self and material possessions. They were given God's financial principles. They have His principles. They fail to obey His principles because they do not trust in Him. Instead, they have developed a pseudo trust in materialism and view themselves as the source of their prosperity. Their issue is not a principle issue. It is an issue of trust in God. As times and seasons repeat themselves, America, much like the nation of Israel, continues the challenge of regaining trust in God.

The nation of Israel was warned many times not to forget God. As recorded in the Bible, they failed to listen, abandoned God, and disregarded his principles. Israel ungratefully turned away from God and embraced the false gods and ungodly traits of other heathen nations. Their disobedience resulted in captivity. An account of their betrayal is recorded in Jeremiah 2.[114] Likewise, Many Americans have wandered away from God and have forgotten about his principles. They have mismanaged the finances God has placed in their care by overextending themselves, and overspending. As a result, disobedience to God's Word has been identified as an accessory to the financial crisis.

As another identifier, many individuals yield to the onslaught of commercial messages in the broadcast media and, due to the lack of self-discipline, succumb to herd behavior. For example, while watching television, viewers are constantly bombarded with a barrage of commercials from companies that have various products for sale and want consumers to know about their products and purchase them. As many watch the manipulative tactics in the advertisements, they fail to realize that they are being influenced to spend money. Before long, they reach for a credit card and make a decision based on impulse and desire with no rationality or logic. Many do not embrace the assumption that when goods and services are paid for with the use of credit cards, although the delayed payments eases the pain experienced when paying cash, the outcome leads to excessive debt caused by overspending. It is always easier to overspend when using a credit card than when using cash. Realizing that they have overspent, many individuals make up excuses to justify their spending. However, justification of actions cannot stop the accumulation of debt. Instead, debt quickly spirals out of control and turns into budget busters.

The issue of not trusting God is compounded with the lack of financial literacy. Regarding the real estate market crash, most individuals did not understand the concept behind a real estate bubble and refused to believe that a bubble existed. They thought the prices of homes would continue to rise with no ceiling. Despite numerous warnings of brewing economic troubles, Americans continued to covet and hoard material

---

[114] Jer. 2.11 & 20: "But my people have exchanged their glorious God for worthless idols . . . My people have committed two sins: They have forsaken me, the spring of living water, and have dug their own cisterns, broken cisterns that cannot hold water . . . Have you not brought this on yourselves by forsaking the Lord your God when he led you in the way? Your wickedness will punish you; your backsliding will rebuke you. Consider then and realize how evil and bitter it is for you when you forsake the Lord your God and have no awe of me," declares the Lord, the Lord Almighty. "Long ago you broke off your yoke and tore off your bonds; you said, "I will not serve you!"

possessions and overspend. They ignored the warning signs of trouble brewing in the financial markets similarly to the residents who lived in the vicinity of Mount Saint Helens.

The fire mountain (Mount Saint Helens) had been in a state of volcanic slumber for almost 125 years. Prior to 1980, it was hard to tell that the mountain was a volcano. Each time the mountain rumbled, the residents of the surrounding areas presumed nothing would happen. They had become immune to the activities of the mountain and simply saw each rumble as another episode of noise that would soon become quiet. The reason they believed that each occurrence would quickly fade into silence was because the episodes of disturbances, marked by the continuous reverberating rolls of what might have sounded like thunder, had been taking place since many of the residents were born. They believed it would remain this way forever.[115]

Prior to the eruption, Mount Saint Helens appeared to be the same as any other fire mountain. In the spring of 1980, the mountain began to rumble. The quakes continued to increase in frequency and size, and before long, ashes and steam began to shoot from the mountain. A bulge developed on the top of the mountain. The bulge signified that something unusual was brewing inside the mountain. Within 4 weeks, the bulge was extremely prominent and continued to grow at about 10 feet per day. On May 18, 1980, at 8:32 a.m., an earthquake occurred about one mile deep down inside the mountain. The constant rattle shook loose the bulge and caused it to collapse, slide down the mountain, and thereby produce the largest historically recorded landslide debris avalanche. Rocks raced down the side of the mountain at speeds of up to 150 miles per hour, creating devastation for miles. Then things got worse. Once the bulge had exploded, the built-up pressure from within the mountain blew off its entire top and 540 tons of volcanic ash covered 22,000 square miles in 11

---

[115] Michael Heilemann, "Today in Earthquake History: Mount St. Helens 1980," University of California, Berkeley Seismological Laboratory. Online: http://seismo.berkeley.edu/blog/seismoblog.php/2010/05/18/today-in-earthquake-history-mount-st-hel-1981 (2 February 2010). The people failed to adhere to the warnings of the eminent dangers that stemmed from the possible eruptions of Mount Saint Helen.

states. Mount Saint Helens was 1300 feet shorter than it was before the blast.[116]

The financial crisis can be compared to the eruption of Mount Saint Helens. Each time the people who lived within the vicinity of the mountain received warning of an impending eruption and saw steam and ashes venting from the mountain, because of previous false alarms, they failed to take the warnings seriously. Likewise, as Americans received warning of potential trouble for the real estate market and saw steam and ashes venting from cracks in the American economy, particularly because of the activities of the mortgage industry, they should have been concerned that there was financial leakage with pending financial hardships. However, many did not have the ability to understand the financial concepts involved, acted like they belonged to a herd of animals, and followed the crowd.[117]

Similar to Mount Saint Helens, the United States economy had spurted steam and ashes in the past and was repeating the behavior. When Burkett saw steam and ashes spurting from the American economy, he predicted that a succession of financial problems would follow.[118] Although most individuals did not realize it, "the finances of America were in shambles and a thin veneer of prosperity covered a festered wound." America was on a real estate production roll. The country was producing more homes than could be consumed.[119] Supply was greater than demand and that caused the prices of homes to drop. The low prices attracted homebuyers. Homeowners transferred their wealth to lenders of high-interest loans at a rate that set a new precedence, while lenders made huge "paper" profits. The majority of borrowers did not understand the nature of the transactions they engaged in. According to Burkett, "it was the era of paper prosperity – the Roaring Twenties, when America could do no wrong."[120] The people of America prospered because of a unique

---

[116] Ibid.

[117] Larry Burkett, *The Coming Economic Earthquake* (Grand Rapids, Michigan: Zondervan, 1994), 15-21.

[118] Ibid, 17. Burkett predicted that "there would be a sudden wave of fiscal responsibility that would sweep over our government; and our politicians would vote to cut spending, cut taxes, cut regulations, and make the free enterprise system function again."

[119] Ibid, 33.

[120] Ibid, 34.

commitment to God's authority. Somehow, they detoured and are traveling down a path that is totally contrary to their original commitment.[121]

A high level of financial illiteracy is another reason America is experiencing a financial crisis. When it comes to financial matters, many individuals have no clue. The effects of the woeful lack of these skills are clearly seen in the lives of many individuals as they continue to make bad choices during the daily courses of their financial dealings. Financial literacy is necessary but, as a standalone, it will not suffice to avert the next financial crisis. Knowing is not enough. Knowledge needs to be coupled with action. Having knowledge of financial literacy will not help individuals if they fail to turn knowledge into action. In other words, acquiring knowledge will not create results unless the knowledge is applied. One of the main inhibitor of turning knowledge into action is people's tendency to equate talking about something with actually doing that thing. Understanding financial concepts and having the knowledge necessary to articulate their process can never equate to actually performing the action steps.[122]

RECOMMENDATIONS

Particularly because of the economically challenging times, if individuals are to be successful at personal finance, there is a great need for financial savvy. Such shrewdness is a bi-product of education in financial literacy. In order to maximize the effectiveness of financial education it is necessary to combine financial education with the action steps necessary to turn financial knowledge into effective actions. Although efforts to promote and increase financial literacy won national support, the knowledge of financial literacy as a "stand-alone," without performing the required activities was found to be somewhat insufficient. Action steps must be combined with knowledge of theories and skills. In other words, knowing

---

[121] Ibid, 40.

[122] Jeffrey Pfeffer and Robert I. Sutton, "The Knowing Doing Gap," Harvard Business School Press, 20 March 2000, 1, 7 & 8. Online: http://toolkitforplcs.pbworks.com/w/file/fetch/40397385/The%20Knowing%20Doing%20Gap.pdf (11 March 2012).

is not enough! The difference between knowing what to do and actually doing it is crucial for successful personal finance. Many individuals who are trained in financial literacy do not apply the knowledge gained to make good choices.

The level of financial literacy and practical money skills that were needed for personal financial management a few decades ago no longer suffice. In order to cope with the ever-changing times, individuals and households also need to change and personal financial management is the primary area where change needs to take place. Without both a spiritual and physical change in the behaviors of individuals and households, the nation will potentially face another time and season of financial crisis and will not be able to circumvent or cope with the challenges while finding a place of solace in God.

In order to fix the nation's deplorable financial situation, Americans must first control the financial matters of their personal lives. They fail to see themselves as part of the problem and believe that the problem lies with the lending institutions and deadbeat mortgage brokers. Instead, they view themselves as typical every-day, normal, regular folks whose financial situations simply spiraled out of control. This may be the case. However, a part of the onus is on Americans to admit their ignorance to financial principles and their need for lessons in financial literacy in order to be able to make better choices, guard against financial pitfalls, and help mitigate future financial crises.

Before each person's situation can be changed, the individual must first change the way he or she views money. Most everyone learn about money from trial and error or from family members. Individuals must become engaged in formal financial literacy education and spend some time learning about money, its source, how it really works, and how to properly manage it. Such principles and skills are not taught during a finance lecture in college. Instead, college students are taught that money is an exact mathematical science, capable of giving accurate results when used in calculations. Students are taught that the better they become at manipulating money, the more of it they will be able to control.

There are a number of individuals with good morals who, despite their positive traits, somehow become entangled in a web of financial troubles of their own making. This occurs because they are ignorant of the characteristics of money. "As a culture (they) are ignorant of what money is and how to handle it. Ignorance is not lack of intelligence; it is lack of knowledge on a particular subject." [123] Ramsey describes money as having two particular attributes. First, he describes money as being active, and likened to a thoroughbred horse that is powerful but, if not trained, will be uncontrollable. Next, Ramsey describes money as having no morals or characteristics. Money is neutral. It is neither good nor bad. In other words, being wealthy does not define an individual as being good or bad. Likewise, being poor does not delineate ones character as good or bad. [124] What individuals do with money is what makes it good or bad. Nonetheless, many individual allow money to gain control of their lives. When individuals get their financial priorities out of order, the inevitable result never fails to be anything other than "money problems." This is an indication that money has become active and has taken over the rein of their lives. However, money problems are never the root problems. Instead, they are the symptoms of the root problem. For example, if an individual is drowning in debt, the bills are the symptoms of a problem. The troubled individual may experience repossession or foreclosure as the consequences of the symptoms. The root problem is the mismanagement of finances as a result of not following financial principles. Many individuals are ignorant of the causes of the problems and also of the financial principles necessary to be applied to their personal finance, in order to be freed from the web of financial mess.

In order to wage war against financial literacy, the government, one of the largest employers, must lead by example. A national financial literacy campaign needs to be run. This campaign must be funded by the government, probably in the form of a stimulus, and must be designed similar to the political campaigns that run just prior to elections. Experts in financial literacy such as Annamarie Lusardi (Dartmouth Professor) and others should head up the campaign. Personal testimonies would be a powerful and extremely effective tool for use during the campaign. Advocates with real life experiences such as individuals who struggled financially as a result of bad financial decision-making but who later

---

[123] Dave Ramsey. *Financial Peace*. (New York: Penguine Group, 2003), 17
[124] Ibid.

received education in financial literacy and are now on their way to success, should be heavily involved in the campaigns. The campaigns should be run in every state and should be aired on every television station, on every radio station, and on the web, including all social media networks. The message coming from the campaign should highlight the nation's rate of financial literacy and detail any relationships between financial literacy and the financial crisis. The logic of the message should be "Hope" for a better tomorrow through education in financial literacy reinforced by personal financial coaching. During the campaign, new and improved financial literacy curricula designed by the government should be advertised. However, because education in financial literacy is a lifelong endeavor, continued education should be offered in the form of personal coaching that is customized to meet the individual's or household's specific goals and needs.

Policy-makers should create the new and improved curricula in financial literacy. The programs should be developed in English, Spanish, and any other dominant languages spoken in America, and should be designed for all ages. After the curricula have been tested for effectiveness, rulemaking authorities should collaborate to mandate stringent rules for education in financial literacy, according to the curricula created by the government. The lessons should be taught in group settings and should also be web-based. As leadership, the government should mandate that employees of all sectors participate in taking the lessons. This can be accomplished similar to all other classes such as sexual harassment and other continuing educational classes that are mandated for governmental employees. Many schools, colleges, and other institutions view financial literacy as a "not-so-important" life skill that does not warrant being taught and has listed the subject somewhere at the bottom of their list of proprieties. Therefore, mandates for offering the program should be placed on financial institutions, schools, colleges, libraries, and employers over whom the policy-makers have jurisdiction. This would include most of the public employees and students. In order to reach the private employees and the unemployed, churches, community centers, libraries, and other publicly- and privately-held organizations and groups should be encouraged to adapt the mandated curricula into programs created and offered to the members of their communities. As incentives for promoting and implementing the financial literacy programs, the publicly- and privately-held firms and other groups should receive funding through government grants, to cover the costs associated with facilitation of the programs.

It is human nature for individuals to desire financial stability and success for their families and themselves. Particularly those who are financially challenged are desperate for a change in their financial lives. As the national campaign progresses, its publicity will cause the desire for education in financial literacy to be captivated by most everyone. Individuals who are financially illiterate will desire more financial education. Those with limited levels of financial knowledge will gain interest in expanding their financial knowledge base. Just as the rate of new home-buyers skyrocketed during the real estate boom, likewise, the desire for financial knowledge will become contagious and spread like wild fire during the campaign.

The low rate of financial literacy among Americans is of concern to many organizations, financial counselors, economists, and consumer advocates. Financial professionals needed to join the campaign can be recruited from among those concerned who received professional training and are qualified to fill the roles of educators. As mentioned earlier, during the national campaign, financial coaching must also be advertised along with financial literacy. After the initial lessons in financial literacy have been taught, many individuals still do not understand their situations, and are not sure of the directions they should be headed in. Many need additional reinforcement. At this point, personal financial coaching must take over. Such tutoring will help individuals and families to realize goals that once seemed impossible, as they progressively understand how to become more successful at personal finance. While being empowered with the right tools for successful personal financial management, that "Hope" for a better tomorrow will be restored to many lives.

Financial coaching can be presented in group settings but will be more effective in one-on-one settings with individuals or families. In order to present financial coaching in group settings, participants in the groups must possess a similar rate of financial knowledge and have similar needs and goals. Many individuals learn faster in group settings as they are able to observe one another and have the opportunity to learn from the personal experiences of others in the group. Depending on the number of participants, some groups may need to have more than one coach. Survey instruments may be constructed and administered to individuals, in order to group like participants. Fast learners in the group may serve as sub-coaches to assist in bringing others up to speed.

Individual coaching should begin at the individual's personal level. In other words, instead of coaching an individual on stocks and bonds knowing quite well that that person has never had any dealings with such investment products, coaching should begin with whatever assets the individual has. For example, the individual may have a demand account (checking, savings, or money market). The coach should make sure the account holder knows all the details of how these accounts work, including any inherent interest rates or potential charges. Other individuals may own pension plans, IRAs, or other types of retirement vehicles. The majority of times, the holders of retirement accounts are unable to articulate the characteristics of their accounts.

The same holds true for mortgage notes. Oftentimes, individuals do not understand how these products work. Pre-purchase counseling should not be an option but should become a mandate for all first-time purchasers and also for individuals and families who purchased homes during the real estate boom, lost their home to foreclosure or short-sale, and are in the process of purchasing another home. Pre-purchase counseling should be recommended for all others. The financial coach may want to break down the mortgage transaction into various segments such as the interest rates, points, or the factors that are included in the overall mortgage payment such as principal, interest, and escrow amounts.

Some individuals may own insurance contracts or may be the beneficiaries. Quite similar to mortgage transaction, most individuals do not fully understand the dynamics of the type(s) of insurance they possess or are entitled to. Many individuals and families do not understand the need for the proper protection through having the right insurances in place and therefore, do not acknowledge the need for insurance. There are a myriad of other financial issues that individuals face. These can all be addressed through, ongoing coaching sessions. Regardless of the nature of the coaching, as knowledge transitions into action, dreams will likewise begin to transition into reality.

The Shifting

THE RECOMMENDATIONS BELOW are based on the conclusions drawn earlier in this chapter. Along with the recommendations above, it is herein recommended that a national three-phase "paradigm shifting" needs to take place. Included in the shifting are a number of important changes that must be effected. If individuals and families do not shift their overall courses of action, they will, most likely, end up where they are headed – to endure another financial dilemma.

A large portion of the financial crisis America is presently experiencing stems from the sins of the nation. When it comes to God's principles, people everywhere are ignorant. In the past, God overlooked people's ignorance regarding His principles. Nowadays, He will not wink at the sins of the nation but instead, commands everyone, everywhere to repent of their sins and turn to Him.[125] The Bible presents a vivid story of how King Jehoshaphat brought revival to his kingdom by sending out teachers to teach the Word of God. The people's minds were renewed and the fear of God fell on everyone, including the surrounding kingdoms.[126] Likewise, the people of America need to turn their hearts to God. He is the God of a second chance who works with individuals despite their shortcomings. His goal is to restore the trust that the people of the American nation once had in him.

THE SHIFTING - PHASE I

America must be restored to its first love. The passion for God that was kindled within the hearts of the Forefathers has been lost and needs to be recovered. The spiritual health of America needs to be improved. This can only be accomplished by first improving the spiritual health of the American people. As stated by George Washington: "It is impossible to

---

[125] Acts 17.30: "And the times of this ignorance God winked at; but now commandeth all men everywhere to repent."
[126] 2 Chr. 17 & 18.

rightly govern . . . without God and the Bible."[127] Whereas the forefathers of the American nation loved and respected God, sought His grace, and called upon him to "aid them in forming a government dedicated to the principle that each individual citizen was answerable to God for his own spiritual life," the generations since that time were and still are self-centered.[128, 129] The Apostle Paul describes individuals who are pre-occupied with self, particularly those of the "me generation," as being stricken with narcissistic personality disorder. He goes on to label those in this group as lovers of money, prideful boasters, blasphemers, unholy, unloving, unthankful individuals who are disobedient to God and parents.[130] The American Pillars of the olden days strongly believed that in order to continue to be a great nation America was dependent on God's protection and leadership. Today, Americans have abandoned God, their source of strength. In order to understand why the nation is enduring the strains of the financial crisis, and to derive any type of remedial actions, Americans need to look back at where the nation began with the founding fathers. As individuals continue to serve God on their terms, greed and its two accomplices, lust and selfishness will continue to plague them. In order to counteract financial and other types of challenges during Phase I of the shifting, a national revival needs to occur. It must be clearly noted,

---

[127] Chuck Edwards, "The Religious Foundation of American Politics: Why Religion and Politics Do Mix." Summit Ministries, 2012. Online: http://www.summit.org/resources/essays/the-religious-foundation-of-american-politics/ (28 March 2012). "A nation that does not remember what it was yesterday, does not know what it is today, nor what it is trying to do. We are trying to do a futile thing if we do not know where we came from or what we have been about. I am absolutely confident that God has blessed our nation in the past because of the righteous goals of our forefathers. Not that they were perfect - they were not - but they built a nation founded on Biblical principles. Many leaders today are attacking those same principles." (Quote by Woodrow Wilson).

[128] Ibid (Quote by Woodrow Wilson).

[129] Gary G. Dull. "A Nation That Forgets God Shall Perish." Online: http://www.fbcaltoona.org/1352108995453560/lib/1352108995453560/_files/A_NATIO N_THAT_FORGETS_GOD_SHALL_PERISH.pdf (19 March 2012).

[130] 2 Tim. 3.1-5, "This know also, that in the last days perilous times shall come. For men shall be lovers of their own selves, covetous, boasters, proud, blasphemers, disobedient to parents, unthankful, unholy, without natural affection, trucebreakers, false accusers, incontinent, fierce, despisers of those that are good, traitors, heady, high-minded, lovers of pleasures more than lovers of God; having a form of godliness, but denying the power thereof: from such turn away."

however, that a revival in the land is not portrayed by a series of meetings during which a visiting evangelist or pastor preaches to gathering crowds, while some weep. A revival in the land means that the men and women of God will in unison humble themselves, pray, seek God's face, and repent while standing in the gap for others. Once this begins among the people of God, the contagion will spread like the fires of the real estate crisis. As and the peoples of the nation turn to God, willingly yield to his will as written in his principles, and relive the motto: "In God We Trust," then and only then will God hear the cries and heal the land as he has promised.[131]

Americans need to understand the supremacy of God and his principles. His absolute supremacy is clearly depicted in the Bible, in both the Old and New Testaments.

> Thine, O LORD is the greatness, and the power, and the glory, and the victory, and the majesty: for all that is in the heaven and in the earth is thine; thine is the kingdom, O LORD, and thou art exalted as head above all. Both riches and honor come of thee, and thou reignest over all; and in thine hand is power and might; and in thine hand it is to make great, and to give strength unto all (1 Chr. 29.11&12).
>
> In whom also we have obtained an inheritance, being predestinated according to the purpose of him who worketh all things after the counsel of his own will (Eph. 1.11).
>
> For of him, and through him, and to him, are all things: to whom be glory forever. Amen (Rom. 11.36).

Once individuals gain heart knowledge (not head knowledge) that God is the Creator and Owner of all things in the universe including all the monies, they will see themselves as stewards or managers of the portion of finances he has placed in their care. As managers of God's finances, individuals are required to operate according to God's written operating procedures as prescribed in his Word. After surrendering to God's will for financial management, the next step individuals must take is to acquaint themselves with God's biblical financial principles. If they truly are cognizant that God is the owner of the finances and see themselves as

---

[131] 2 Chr. 7.14: "If my If my people, which are called by my name, shall humble themselves, and pray, and seek my face, and turn from their wicked ways; then will I hear from heaven, and will forgive their sin, and will heal their land."

stewards, they will have a clearer understanding of what is expected of them and many will spontaneously create budgets and be more careful about how they spend, save, and give. Those who fail to grasp the knowledge of who God really is will continue to mistrust him. This lack of trust in God will lead to continued mismanagement of the finances God has placed them as stewards over and as a result, they will continue to endure financial struggles.[132] If the people of the great nation of America fail to turn back to God and once again place their trust in him, the consequences can be potentially devastating. The Bible states: "The wicked shall be turned into hell, and all the nations that forget God" (Ps. 9.17).

THE SHIFTING - PHASE II

The heightened awareness for education in financial literacy needs to be taken to the next level. The greatest starting place for such a lifelong process is at home. Children who are not already receiving allowances should be given allowances and allowed to make financial decisions with the guidance of their parents. Also, more funding should be appropriated for research in this area and special funding should be allocated for more in-depth evaluations of many of the existing programs, to test their effectiveness. Some programs will need to be discontinued while others will need to be revised. Designing and implementing an extensive campaign to promote financial literacy can also accomplish heightened awareness. The desire to know is a natural tendency. Some individuals acknowledge their inadequacies in personal finance and desire to gain financial knowledge. Whereas, others with limited financial knowledge are unaware of their deficiency and therefore, do not realize that they need help in that area. As a result, they do not seek help. In order to arouse most everyone's interest in financial literacy and hype individuals about becoming engaged in the subject, commercials that advertise financial literacy training should be aired on both radio and television, as often as food commercials are aired. Such commercials may include advertising transformation seminars that are planned to take place at

---

[132] Hos. 4.6: "My people perish for lack of knowledge."

churches, community centers, libraries, schools, and workplaces, among other settings. Behavioral Finance needs to be introduced during the seminars, to teach individuals that they do not have to adapt the mentality of the "Hiltons" or the "Jones" especially when it does not fit within the parameters of their lifestyles.

Policy makers need to create more stringent policies that call for mandatory education in financial literacy and practical money skills for everyone, including youths and seniors. Although financial literacy may already be embedded in an institution's curricula, it can be heightened through collaboration of the public and private sectors. Field trips to banks and credit Unions or to the Federal Reserve might be instituted as a result of partnership efforts. Credits earned from these lessons should become a graduation requirement. Curriculums need to be revised to include new and improved teaching methods that explain the characteristics of the complex financial products that are constantly making their entrance into the financial markets.

Prior to the start of the financial lessons, a sense of the students' determination to learn and willingness to change their financial management habits should be evaluated. This pre-test can be structured in the form of surveys. The 6 stages of the Transtheoretical Model of Behavior Change can be used as a guideline against which the level of the student's desire to change is measured. Following are the 6 stages:

1) Preparation – individuals do not intend to change in the near future
2) Contemplation – individuals begin to recognize they have a problem
3) Preparation – individuals intend to take action
4) Action – individuals begin to modify their actions
5) Maintenance – individuals have changed their behaviors
6) Termination – individuals have completed behavioral change[133]

---

[133] James O. Prochaska, John C. Norcross, Carlo C. DiClemente. *Changing for Good: A Revolutionary Six-Stage Program for Overcoming Bad Habits and Moving Your Life Positively Forward.* (New York: Harper Collins Publishers, 2002) 15.

THE SHIFTING - PHASE III

In this third and final stage of the shifting, individuals must avail themselves to learn the financial lessons taught and be disciplined to follow through with the necessary action steps to transform knowledge into action. However money management problems are not always grounded in the lack of financial knowledge. Oftentimes, financial problems are the symptoms of rooted behavioral problems. For individuals with limited financial knowledge, the shifting must change from not knowing to knowing. For individuals who are savvy regarding financial knowledge yet fail to successfully manage their finances, the shifting must change from knowing to doing, as knowledge is shifted into action. The power of transforming knowledge into action is extremely vital at this point. This change requires self-discipline and will-power.

When teaching financial literacy, educators including parents should include topics on self-control. Educators need to understand some of the characteristics of human behavior, particularly why individuals act in the ways that they do. Individuals are free moral agents with free wills. However, they still need to exercise their free wills in a responsible, disciplined manner. One of the fruits of the spirit is self-control (temperance).[134] A person does not simply decide to become disciplined. It takes the Holy Spirit and the grace of God to make this happen. Once self-control is produced by the Holy Spirit in the life on an individual, that person is empowered for success in all areas of life, including personal financial management. When Americans everywhere humble themselves, confess their sins, seek the face of the Lord, and turn from their wicked ways, then and only then will God hear from heaven and will heal/restore their land. God will also restore all the years of financial leanness. It is at this point of restoration that God's wish that his children prosper and be in good health even as their souls prosper will be materialized.[135]

---

[134] Gal. 5.2 & 3: "But the fruit of the Spirit is love, joy, peace, longsuffering, gentleness, goodness, faith, meekness, temperance: against such there is no law."
[135] 3 Jn. 1.2: "Beloved, I wish above all things that thou mayest prosper and be in health, even as thy soul prospereth."

A Final Thought

IT IS BECAUSE OF THE mercies of God that the nation of America is not consumed.[136] As the American nation continues to prayerfully make its way through the financial crisis tunnel, there is hope! There is a light at the end of the tunnel! The light can be seen entering the tunnel through the opening at the far end. There is only one way of escape from all of the financial mess. Jesus Christ is the way, the truth and the life.[137] He invites everyone to stop fumbling in the dark tunnel, come back to the love they once knew, and place their trust in the God of the founding fathers. As prophesied by Malachi, the nation has strayed away from God's ordinances. The people have failed to obey his Word and have not kept his principles. He beckons to the nation to return unto Him and he will return unto them.[138] God promised to restore the years that have been eaten up by the various crises. He also promised that his children will never be ashamed.[139] This does not mean that there will not be any type of financial difficulties. Challenges will come. However, if individuals are trained in financial literacy and living according to biblical principles, they will be able to shift gears, make adjustments, avert the challenges before they become crises, and thereby *"Overcome Financial Invasion."* Everyone's finances will be in order. As people turn their hearts back to God in repentance, there will be a national revival. In return for obedience to the Word of God, Americans will be blessed with prosperous long lives.[140]

---

[136] Lam. 3.22: "It is of the Lord's mercies that (America is) not consumed because His compassions fail not."

[137] Jn. 14.6: "Jesus saith unto him, I am the way, the truth, and the life: no man cometh unto the Father, but by me."

[138] Mal. 3.7: "Even from the days of your fathers ye are gone away from Mine ordinances, and have not kept them. Return to Me, and I will return unto you; saith the Lord of host."

[139] Joel 2.25 & 26: "And I will restore to you the years that the locust hath eaten, the cankerworm, and the caterpillar, and the palmerworm, my great army which I sent among you. And ye shall eat in plenty, and be satisfied, and praise the name of the Lord your God, that hath dealt wondrously with you: and my people shall never be ashamed."

[140] Deut. 5.32 & 33: "Ye shall observe to do therefore as the Lord your God hath commanded you: ye shall not turn aside to the right hand or to the left. Ye shall walk in

Also, God has promised to give all those who trust in him new hearts and spirits that they will be able to turn their lives around and live.[141] God is not slack, concerning his promises.[142] He is faithful regarding his promises.[143]

---

all the ways which the Lord your God hath commanded you, that ye may live, and that it may be well with you, and that ye may prolong your days in the land which ye shall possess."

[141] Ezek. 18.31&32: "Cast away from you all your transgressions, whereby ye have transgressed; and make you a new heart and a new spirit: for why will ye die, O house of Israel? For I have no pleasure in the death of him that dieth, saith the Lord God: wherefore turn yourselves, and live ye."

[142] 2 Pet. 3.9: "The Lord is not slack concerning his promise, as some men count slackness."

[143] Heb. 10.23: "Let us hold fast the profession of our faith without wavering; for He is faithful that promised."

The alarm has been sounded.

The message has been delivered.

Will you embrace God's principles of finance?

References

Adamu, Abdul. *The Effects of the Global Crisis on Nigerian Economy.* Online: http://www.rrojasdatabank.info/crisisdb/onnigeria09.pdf (Retrieved August 10, 2011).

Annual Report. (2007). The Federal Reserve Bank of San Francisco: *The Subprime Mortgage Market.* Online: http://www.frbsf.org/publications/federalreserve/annual/2007/subprime.pdf. (Retrieved 26 August 2011).

Barton, David. (2008). *The Founding Fathers on Jesus, Christianity and the Bible.* Online: http://www.wallbuilders.com/libissuesarticles.asp?id=8755 (Retrieved 18 March 2012).

Bianco, Katalina, M. (2008). *The Subprime Lending Crisis: Causes and Effects of the Mortgage Meltdown.* Online: http://www.business.cch.com/bankingfinance/focus/news/Subprime_WP_rev.pdf. (Retrieved 28 May 2011).

Boa, Kenneth. *Stewardship: Your Time, Talent, and Treasure.* Online: http://www.kenboa.org/downloads/pdf/1-Stewardship.pdf. (Retrieved 16 March 2012).

Burkett, Larry. (1994). *The Coming Economic Earthquake.* Grand Rapids, Michigan: Zondervan.

Burkett, Larry. (1993). *Your Finances in Changing Times.* Chicago: Moody Press.

Cohen, M., McGuiness, E., Sebstad, J., and Stack, K. (2006). *Financial Education: From Poverty to Prosperity.* Online: http://microfinanceopportunities.org/docs/Market_Research_for_Financial_Education.pdf (Retrieved 25 March 2012).

Cole, Shaw, Sampson, Thomas, and Zia, Bilah. (2010). *Prices or Knowledge? What Drives Demand for Financial Services in Emerging Markets?* Online: http://www.hbs.edu/research/pdf/09-117.pdf. (Retrieved 2 August 2011).

Economist, The. (16 June 2005). *The Global Housing Boom: In Come the Waves.* Online: http://www.economist.com/node/4079027. (Retrieved 15 January 2012).

Chuck Edwards. (2012). *The Religious Foundation of American Politics: Why Religion and Politics Do Mix.* Online: http://www.summit.org/resources/essays/the-religious-foundation-of-american-politics/ (Retrieved 1 August 2012).

Emerson, Michael, Foote, Jill, and Long Elizabeth. (2006). *The Effectiveness of Financial Literacy Seminars.* Online: http://www.thewomensresource.org/pdf/Financial_Literacy_Report_2006.pdf (Retrieved August 1, 2012).

Family Services Center. (2004). *The Need for Financial Literacy.* Online: http://www.fsc-hsv.org/moneymgt-finliteracy.htm. (Retrieved 2 August 2011).

FDIC National Survey of Unbanked and Underbanked Households. (2009). *Executive Summary.* Online: http://www.fdic.gov/householdsurvey/executive_summary.pdf. (Retrieved 15 August 2011).

FINRA Education Investor Foundation. *Financial Capabilities in the United States.* Online: http://www.finrafoundation.org/web/groups/foundation/@foundation/documents/foundation/p120535.pdf. (Retrieved 15 January 2012).

Financial Literacy and Education Commission. (2010). *Why and How: Background Report Developing the 2011 National Strategy.* Online: http://www.mymoney.gov/sites/default/files/downloads/National%20Strategy%20Background.pdf. (Retrieved 20 July 2011).

Goldberg, Joachim and Von Nitzsch, Rudiger. (2001). *Behavioral Finance.* New York: John Wiley and Sons, Inc.

Government Accountability Office. (2011). *The Federal Government's Role in Empowering Americans to Make Sound Financial Choices.* Online: http://www.gao.gov/new.items/d11504t.pdf. (Retrieved 1 August 2011).

Hall, Alice J. (July 1975). *Benjamin Franklin, Philosopher of Dissent.* National Geographic Magazine, Vol., 148, No. 1, :94.

Harnisch, Thomas L. (2010). Perspectives. American Association of State Colleges and Universities. Online: http://www.congressweb.com/aascu/docfiles/AASCU_Perspectives_Boosting_Financial_Literacy.pdf. (Retrieved 11 August 2011).

Henry, Matthew. *The Matthew Henry Study Bible.* King James Version. USA: World Bible, Copyright 1994 by World Bible Publishers, Inc. Print.

Junior Achievement. "Teens and Careers Survey," Executive Summary, 2010. Online: http://www.ja.org/ (31 July 2012).

Jump$tart Coalition for Personal Financial Literacy. (2007). *National Standards in K-12 Personal Finance Education*. Online: *http://www.jumpstart.org/assets/files/standard_book-ALL.pdf* (Retrieved 5 January 2012).

Kilmister, Andy. (December 2008). *The Economic Crisis and its Effects*. International *Viewpoint*, IV407, 6. Online: http://www.internationalviewpoint.org/IMG/pdf/IV407.pdf (Retrieved 11 August 2011).

King James Version / Amplified Bible / Parallel Bible. Grand Rapids, Michigan: Zondervan, Copyright 1987 by the Lockman Foundation. Print.

Kiviat, Barbara and Morduch Jonathan. (2012). *From Financial Literacy to Financial Action*. www.mcgraw-hillresearchfoundation.org. (Retrieved 18 March 2012).

Kluth, Brian. *Biblical and Financial Insights Into Generosity and Finances*. Online: http://www.kluth.org/people/bookchapter.htm. (Retrieved 18 March 2012).

Lacko, James, M. and Pappalardo, Janis, K. *Improving Consumer Mortgage Disclosures: An Empirical of Current and Prototype Disclosure Forms*. Online: http://www.ftc.gov/os/2007/06/P025505MortgageDisclosureexecutivesummary.pdf. (Retrieved 15 August 2011).

Lendnal, Andrew. (2011). *Gold Start: Teaching Your Child About Money*. New Zealand: Exisle Publishing Limited.

Lusardi, Annamaria. (2008). *Financial Literacy: An Essential Tool for Informed Consumer Choice?* Online: http://www.dartmouth.edu/~alusardi/Papers/Lusardi_Informed_Consumer.pdf. (Retrieved 14 July 2011).

Miller, Joe, and Jackson, Brooks. (2008). Fact Check.Org. *Who Caused the Economic Crisis?* Online: http://factcheck.org/2008/10/who-caused-the-economic-crisis/. (Retrieved August 28, 2011).

Morris, Kenneth M. and Morris, Virginia B. (2000). *Guide to Understanding Personal Finance*. New York: Lightbulb Press.

Osak, Michelle. (8 July 2010). *Behavioral Economics 101: Influencing Consumer Choice.* Financial Post. Online: http://business.financialpost.com/2010/07/08/behavioral-economics-101-influencing-customer-choice/ (Retrieved 18 March 2012).

Pfeffer, Jeffrey and Sutton, Robert I. (2000). *The Knowing Doing Gap.* Online: http://toolkitforplcs.pbworks.com/w/file/fetch/40397385/The%20Knowing%20Doing%20Gap.pdf . (Retrieved 20 March 2000).

President's Advisory Council on Financial Literacy. (2008). *2008 Annual Report to the President.* Online: http://www.financialeducationbook.com/making-bank-book/wp-content/uploads/2011/03/PACFL_ANNUAL_REPORT_1_16_09.pdf (Retrieved 5 July 2011).

Prochaska, James O., Norcross, John C., DiClemente, Carlo C. (1995). *Changing for Good: A Revolutionary Six-Stage Program for Overcoming Bad Habits and Moving Your Life Positively Forward.* U.S.A.: William Morrow Paperbacks.

Ramsey, Dave, L, III. (2003). *Financial Peace.* New York: Viking.

Ramsey, David, L, III. (2008). *Financial Peace University Workbook.* Brentwood, Tennessee: The Lampo Group, Inc.

Ramsey, Dave, L, III. (2009). *The Total Money Makeover.* Tennessee: Thomas Nelson.

Semommung, Ben. (2011). *Discover the Power of Financial Education!* Online: http://ultimateallowancebook.com/blog/?p=297. (Retrieved 7 July 2011).

Shiller, Robert J. (2008). *The Subprime Solution: How Today's Global Financial Crisis Happened, and What to do About It.* Princeton, NJ: Princeton University Press. Online: http://www.afi.es/EO/The%20Subprime%20Solution%20-%20Shiller,%202008.pdf (Retrieved 21 August 2011).

Sovern, Jeff (2010). *Preventing Future Economic Crises Through Consumer Protection Law or How the Truth-in-Lending Act Failed the Subprime Borrowers.* Online: http://moritzlaw.osu.edu/lawjournal/issues/volume71/number4/sovern.pdf (Retrieved 2 July 2011).

Twight. Dana. ((2008). *Getting Our Money's Worth: Exploring State Strategies for Investing in Financial Literacy Education.* Online: http://feppp.org/pdf/state-strategies.pdf (Retrieved 5 August 2011).

Xiao, Jing J., O'Neill, Barbara, Prochaska, Janice M., Kerbel, Claudia, Brennan, Patricia, & Bristow, Barbara Bristow. (2001): Vol. 47. *Application of the Transtheoretical Model of Change to Financial Behaviors.* Online: http://165.230.176.46/money2000/pdfs/acci01m2k-proceedings.pdf (Retrieved 30 May 2012).